Turkey, the Arab Spring and Beyond

T0346602

It has been almost five years now since a new collective consciousness of Arab masses transformed the political landscape of the Middle East and North Africa. In just a short period of time, the people of the Arab world protested against their rulers, putting an end to long-time authoritarian leaders in Tunisia, Egypt, Libya, and Yemen, while bringing others to the eve of collapse. Although the uprisings were initially successful, the people's strong will to see honour, dignity, rights, and good governance realized within their respective countries was fiercely combated by the ruling strata of these states and their strategies to ensure authoritarian survival.

The changing political landscape and the dynamic processes of the Arab Spring have caught the attention of academics as well. There is a blossoming literature being written on the Arab Spring focusing on social protests, authoritarian resilience and learning, opposition strategies, the rise of non-state actors, state failure, foreign policy, and the new geopolitical landscape. Therefore, with the desire to contribute to this literature, this edited volume aims to address the changing political atmosphere and the challenges of the emerging geopolitical order, particularly focusing on Turkish foreign policy and its response to the Arab Spring.

This book was originally published as a special issue of the *Journal of Balkan and Near Eastern Studies*.

Bülent Aras is Professor of International Relations, Sabancı University and Global Fellow at Wilson Center. He was the head of the Diplomatic Academy and Center for Strategic Research at Turkey's Ministry of Foreign Affairs. His recent publications include *War in the Gardens of Babylon: Middle East after the Iraqi War* (2004), *Turkey and the Greater Middle East* (2004), and *September 11 and World Politics: American Hegemony Reconsidered* (2004).

E. Fuat Keyman is Director of the Istanbul Policy Center and Professor of International Relations at Sabancı University. Recent publications include *Hegemony through Transformations; Democracy, Identity, and Foreign Policy in Turkey* (2014), and *Symbiotic Antagonism: Competing Nationalisms in Turkey* (With Ayşe Kadioğlu; 2011).

Turkey, the Arab Spring and Beyond

Edited by
Bülent Aras and E. Fuat Keyman

LONDON AND NEW YORK

First published 2017
by Routledge

2 Park Square, Milton Park, Abingdon, Oxfordshire OX14 4RN
711 Third Avenue, New York, NY 10017

Routledge is an imprint of the Taylor & Francis Group, an informa business

First issued in paperback 2018

British Library Cataloguing in Publication Data
A catalogue record for this book is available from the British Library

ISBN: 978-1-138-64306-2 (hbk)
ISBN: 978-0-367-02842-8 (pbk)

Typeset in Minion Pro
by RefineCatch Limited, Bungay, Suffolk

Publisher's Note
The publisher accepts responsibility for any inconsistencies that may have
arisen during the conversion of this book from journal articles to book chapters,
namely the possible inclusion of journal terminology.

Disclaimer
Every effort has been made to contact copyright holders for their permission to
reprint material in this book. The publishers would be grateful to hear from any
copyright holder who is not here acknowledged and will undertake to rectify
any errors or omissions in future editions of this book.

Contents

Citation Information   vii

1. Turkey, the Arab Spring and Beyond   1
   Bülent Aras and E. Fuat Keyman

2. Mediation as a Foreign Policy Tool in the Arab Spring: Turkey, Qatar and Iran   4
   Pınar Akpınar

3. Reform and Capacity Building in the Turkish Foreign Ministry: Bridging the
   Gap between Ideas and Institutions   21
   Bülent Aras

4. Practical Geopolitical Reasoning in the Turkish and Qatari Foreign Policy on
   the Arab Spring   38
   Özgür Pala and Bülent Aras

5. The Impact of the Arab Spring on the Gulf Cooperation Council   55
   Larbi Sadiki

6. Turkey and Iran: The Two Modes of Engagement in the Middle East   73
   E. Fuat Keyman and Onur Sazak

7. Turkish Foreign Policy towards the Arab Spring: Between Western Orientation
   and Regional Disorder   89
   Emirhan Yorulmazlar and Ebru Turhan

Index   105

Citation Information

The chapters in this book were originally published in the *Journal of Balkan and Near Eastern Studies*, volume 17, issue 3 (September 2015). When citing this material, please use the original page numbering for each article, as follows:

Chapter 1
Introduction to the Special Issue: Turkey, the Arab Spring and Beyond
Bülent Aras and E. Fuat Keyman
Journal of Balkan and Near Eastern Studies, volume 17, issue 3 (September 2015)
pp. 249–251

Chapter 2
Mediation as a Foreign Policy Tool in the Arab Spring: Turkey, Qatar and Iran
Pınar Akpınar
Journal of Balkan and Near Eastern Studies, volume 17, issue 3 (September 2015)
pp. 252–268

Chapter 3
Reform and Capacity Building in the Turkish Foreign Ministry: Bridging the Gap between Ideas and Institutions
Bülent Aras
Journal of Balkan and Near Eastern Studies, volume 17, issue 3 (September 2015)
pp. 269–285

Chapter 4
Practical Geopolitical Reasoning in the Turkish and Qatari Foreign Policy on the Arab Spring
Özgür Pala and Bülent Aras
Journal of Balkan and Near Eastern Studies, volume 17, issue 3 (September 2015)
pp. 286–302

Chapter 5
The Impact of the Arab Spring on the Gulf Cooperation Council
Larbi Sadiki
Journal of Balkan and Near Eastern Studies, volume 17, issue 3 (September 2015)
pp. 303–320

Chapter 6

Turkey and Iran: The Two Modes of Engagement in the Middle East
E. Fuat Keyman and Onur Sazak
Journal of Balkan and Near Eastern Studies, volume 17, issue 3 (September 2015)
pp. 321–336

Chapter 7

Turkish Foreign Policy towards the Arab Spring: Between Western Orientation and Regional Disorder
Emirhan Yorulmazlar and Ebru Turhan
Journal of Balkan and Near Eastern Studies, volume 17, issue 3 (September 2015)
pp. 337–352

For any permission-related enquiries please visit:
http://www.tandfonline.com/page/help/permissions

Turkey, the Arab Spring and Beyond

Bülent Aras and E. Fuat Keyman

It has been almost five years now since a new collective consciousness of Arab masses transformed the political landscape of the Middle East and North Africa. In just a short period of time, the people of the Arab world protested against their rulers, putting an end to long-time authoritarian leaders in Tunisia, Egypt, Libya and Yemen, while bringing others to the eve of collapse. Although the uprisings were initially successful, the people's strong will to see honour, dignity, rights and good governance realized within their respective countries was fiercely combated by the ruling strata of these states and their strategies to ensure authoritarian survival. This dialectical struggle put an end to early optimist accounts and paved the way for speculations that the Arab Spring had come to an end. However, before we can speculate what a precise ending to the uprisings will look (or had looked) like, it must first be asked, what is the destiny of the Arab Spring?

The political landscape does not always present a clear or promising picture, however, the question of the destiny of the Arab Spring corresponds to some reality on the ground. On the one hand, there is a general consensus that the worst has yet to be seen. The rise of non-state actors, cross-border re-territorialization and the search for state-like entities, sectarian conflicts, proxy wars and state failure paint a bleak picture for the future of these countries. On the other hand, there is a new psychological threshold for resisting authoritarian rule and an emerging collective consciousness to change the political landscape for the betterment of political rights and good governance. Although it seems that there will be some challenging periods ahead, revolution is a difficult process, and it is certainly not over. The Arab masses have bridged the time lag between their authoritarian setting and current world realities, and they are not likely to accept anything less than what the rest of the world has asked for in terms of seeing international standards of human dignity and rights realized in their homeland.

The changing political landscape and the dynamic processes of the Arab Spring have caught the attention of academics as well. There is a blossoming literature being written on the Arab Spring focusing on social protests, authoritarian resilience and learning, opposition strategies, the rise of non-state actors, state failure, foreign policy and the new geopolitical landscape. Therefore, with the desire to contribute to this literature, this special issue aims to address the changing political atmosphere and the challenges of the emerging geopolitical order, particularly focusing on Turkish foreign policy and its response to the Arab Spring.

This special issue is a part of our research on the Arab Spring, namely, POMEAS (Project on the Middle East and Arab Spring), at Istanbul Policy Center, Sabancı University. For this issue we have chosen to focus on recent changes in Turkish foreign policy, Turkey's policy toward the Arab Spring, its engagement and interaction with regional developments, Turkey's relations with Qatar and Iran, and the overlapping and conflicting policies of Turkey, Qatar and Iran on the Arab Spring.

Bülent Aras discusses the transformation of Turkish foreign policy, taking the changes in the structure of Turkey's Foreign Ministry as a case study. Turkey's institutional adaptation of its foreign policy framework is exemplary in showing that policymakers have indeed succeeded in bridging the gap between ideas and institutions to some extent. Aras points out that despite considerable progress, work still needs to be done toward the institutional adaptation of the idealistic perspective of foreign policy.

Emirhan Yorulmazlar and Ebru Turhan discuss the orientation of Turkish foreign policy in the Arab Spring. They argue that Turkish foreign policy is caught in between regional disorder and Western disengagement from the region; meanwhile, Turkey is trying to reconcile its own Western orientation and regional priorities. Yorulmazlar and Turhan suggest an alternative foreign policy trajectory to preserve an active policy in the post-Arab Spring atmosphere.

E. Fuat Keyman and Onur Sazak discuss both the Turkish and the Iranian modes of engagement in the Arab Spring. In the Iranian case, the mode has relied on resistance to change in the region, as well as at home. In the Turkish case, there has been a more positive attitude towards regional transformation in the region. To reconcile these two modes, Keyman and Sazak suggest that each country follow a trajectory toward resolving their domestic problems and engage in the region through ethical, moral and constructive values.

Özgür Pala and Bülent Aras utilize the concept of geographic reasoning to explain the convergence in Turkish and Qatari policies toward the Arab Spring. According to Pala and Aras, Qatar's new activism is the result of its search for a regional role, while Turkey's various engagements aim to secure an international position at large. They conclude that Turkey and Qatar, despite minor differences, seem to have matured their partnership despite shifting alliances.

Pınar Akpınar focuses on another level of Turkish, Iranian and Qatari involvement in the Arab Spring, namely, each country's mediation effort to solve the conflicts in the new emerging political environment. She examines why and how these states mediate and argues that their attempt to present themselves as effective mediators has achieved different results. Akpınar concludes that the sustainability of this role in each country's foreign policy depends on their commitment and reliability as mediators.

Larbi Sadiki contextualizes the change after the Arab Spring, addressing how politics is organized in the Arab political landscape. He puts a specific focus on Qatar's response, having the Gulf Cooperation Council's 'story' at the background, to the Arab Spring.

Mediation as a Foreign Policy Tool in the Arab Spring: Turkey, Qatar and Iran

Pınar Akpınar

This paper investigates to what extent mediation has been a relevant foreign policy tool during the Arab Spring by looking into the mediation attempts of Turkey, Qatar and Iran. To answer this question, the paper examines why and how these actors mediated, to what extent they were able to apply mediation as a tool of foreign policy, whether their mediation attempts could deliver any results and whether there was a receptive audience with respect to their mediation. Despite certain setbacks, mediation has been a relevant foreign policy tool during the Arab Spring. The uses of mediation by these actors run parallel to their foreign policy priorities. In addition, during the Arab Spring, mediation has proved more effective in small-scale conflicts, such as hostage crises, rather than large-scale ones, such as those between regimes and oppositions. Despite considerable potential for regional powers to take on mediator roles, the effectiveness of their mediation attempts depends on their commitment and reliability as mediators.

Introduction

The Arab Spring has triggered several disputes in the Middle East that have been multidimensional in nature, often involving issues of ideology, identity, territory, sovereignty and resources. These have been intrastate, asymmetric, low-intensity conflicts that are unpredictable and difficult—if not impossible—to fight by conventional ways. The Arab Spring also witnessed the emergence of several factions and new actors within the opposition, all entering the stage with different interests and positions. The deepening gap among different factions fuelled fears and fed the attitude of 'survive or vanish'. This understanding encouraged the use of violence, making the conflicts even more complicated by threatening the security even of countries that have not directly experienced the Arab Spring such as Turkey, Iran and Qatar.

The fall and the weakening of the regimes during the Arab Spring resulted in a gap of authority in the region. This gap was further widened as a result of the rivalries between regional powers fuelling sectarian disputes and radicalism. Different forms of conflict resolution ranging from military intervention to non-violent methods have been applied over the course of the Arab Spring. As a result of its complexity and the multiplicity of the actors, conventional tools have proved ineffective, and mediation has once again come onto the stage as a tool of non-violent conflict resolution.

A number of actors took on mediator roles, some of which have been fruitful while others have proved ineffective. The already-existing doubt and mistrust against the West, coupled with Western reluctance to intervene in the conflicts pertaining to the Arab Spring, created room for regional actors such as Qatar, Turkey and Iran to take on more active roles in regional disputes. This paper analyses the mediation attempts made by these actors aiming to understand to what extent mediation is still a relevant policy tool within the context of the Arab Spring. In order to answer that question, the paper will examine why and how these actors mediated, to what extent they were able to apply mediation as a tool of foreign policy, whether their mediation attempts could deliver any results and whether there was a receptive audience with respect to their mediation.

Mediation as a Tool of Foreign Policy

Definitions of mediation vary across the literature. According to the United Nations (UN), mediation is 'a process whereby a third party assists two or more parties, with their consent, to prevent, manage or resolve a conflict by helping them to develop mutually acceptable agreements'.[1] While some scholars emphasize the importance of voluntary presence and mutual consent of the parties during mediation,[2] others underpin the non-binding nature of the process indicating the lack of force and authority of the third party.[3]

The literature depicts an ideal mediator as a neutral entity that lacks any prior interest in the outcome of a mediation process. As such, neutrality is a primary principle in mediation. However, the literature largely ignores the fact that when the mediator is a state, mediation often becomes a tool of foreign policy, if not the foreign policy itself. As underpinned by Ramsbotham *et al.*, 'governments are not always willing to shoulder a mediating role when their national interests are not at stake, and, where they are, mediation readily blurs into traditional diplomacy and statecraft'.[4]

Touval criticizes the understanding of international mediation 'as an autonomous activity that is impacted by politics but is not part of politics' and rather suggests that mediation should be considered 'as part of foreign policy'[5] when practised by states. As such, there is a tendency in the literature to refer to international mediation as a solitary and rather technical activity in isolation from the surrounding political context. In this view, 'the mediator's perceptions of the international system', 'its domestic needs' and 'its foreign policy objectives and strategies' are influential in determining the role of a state as a mediator.[6] This whole orientation eventually affects the outcome of a mediation process.

A state's ultimate goal as a mediator, in this sense, may not always be solely altruism or to end a conflict but to achieve its foreign policy goals. As Wall suggests, 'to enhance his reputation or to please his constituency' may be the goal of a mediator.[7] While this goal may sometimes be just to end a human tragedy, as Kamrava notes, it may as well be strengthening a state's regional role, enhancing its legitimacy, image or prestige in the international arena.[8] At times, it may even be used as a 'survival strategy'.[9] In other words, the success of a mediation process may sometimes be 'subordinate to the mediating state's primary domestic and foreign policy concerns'.[10] When the mediator is a state, 'mediation may well be seen as the continuation of foreign policy by other means'.[11]

This study considers mediation as a tool of foreign policy. It argues that when the mediator is a state, mediation often becomes a tool of exerting its interests. This has been an apparent case during the Arab Spring when a number of states took on mediator roles to exert their interests and expand their sphere of influence in the region. Building on this theoretical discussion, this paper will analyse the mediation attempts by Qatar, Iran and Turkey within the context of the Arab Spring. It will try to understand how and why these actors used mediation as a foreign policy tool, what have been the main challenges for their mediator roles and to what extent mediation is still a relevant tool of foreign policy for these states.

Turkey as a Mediator during the Arab Spring

Turkey's mediator role has come to the fore in a number of conflicts during the Arab Spring, including in Bahrain, Libya, Syria, Iraq and lately in Yemen. Turkey mediated to end the crisis in Bahrain in 2011 by exchanging communication with a number of parties including Saudi Arabia, Iran and the United Arab Emirates, as well as the Bahraini state and the opposition groups. It called on the government to consider reforms, the opposition to refrain from violence and the parties to prevent sectarian conflict.[12] Its mediation attempt achieved partial results by initiating communication among the parties. Bahrain is also one of the very few countries where Turkey followed a neutral position during the Arab Spring.

In Libya, Turkey made three mediation attempts. First, it mediated the release of four *New York Times* journalists in March 2011 who were briefly detained by Qaddafi forces.[13] Second, a journalist from the *Guardian*, Ghait Abdulahad, who had been detained by the Libyan authorities, was also released through Turkey's mediation in March 2011.[14] Turkey's mediation in these cases came at a time when both the USA and the UK had summoned their diplomatic representatives from Libya due to security concerns and were represented by the Turkish Embassy. As a result, they requested Turkey's mediation, and in both cases, its mediation achieved results.

Turkey also mediated between the Gaddafi government and the Transitional National Council in Libya. Its proposal entailed a threefold strategy of conflict resolution in Libya, which included a ceasefire, commencing political dialogue between the government and the opposition, and running democratic elections.[15] However, its mediation faced severe challenges since it took place alongside the NATO (North Atlantic Treaty Organization) military intervention into the country. At the onset of the conflict, Turkey positioned itself against a military intervention in Libya. Erdoğan accused the international community of acting 'out of oil concerns' and called on them 'to act with conscience, justice, laws and universal humane values'.[16] Erdoğan reiterated that unless peace is achieved, Libya could turn into a 'second Iraq' or 'another Afghanistan'.[17] This call was attributed to, according to some circles, Ankara's close ties with the regime of former President of Libya Muammar Gaddafi and the $15 billion worth of Turkish businesses in Libya.[18] As a result, Turkey was not invited to the meeting of coalition forces in Paris, and a military intervention ensued in Libya.[19]

Turkey's efforts to mediate amid the NATO military campaign were perceived with discomfort by the NATO forces. Turkey was accused of sidelining both the Libyan government and the opposition. For instance, a group from the Libyan opposition protested Turkey's refusal to arm the opposition in front of the Turkish consulate in Benghazi while the Turkish Red Crescent, a semi-governmental aid organization, was docking in Benghazi.[20] Furthermore, the closure of the Turkish Embassy in Tripoli on 2 May 2011 for security reasons had a negative impact on Turkey's mediator role as well.[21] Subsequently, Turkey changed its position on Libya and called on Gaddafi to step down. As a result, Turkey's efforts in Libya were criticized by its Western allies, the Libyan government and the opposition.

In addition to the Libyan case, Turkey also organized facilitation meetings by bringing together Sunni leaders such as the Speaker of the Iraqi Parliament Salim al-Jabouri, Vice-President of Iraq Usama al-Nujayfi and the Secretary-General of the Iraqi Islamic Party Ayad al-Samarrai. It also mediated between the Sunni and Shia Turkmen leaders from Tel Afar on 24–28 February 2011 in Istanbul, which resulted in an agreement.[22]

Turkey also proposed mediation in Syria. At the onset of the Syrian uprisings, Turkey's then Foreign Minister and current Prime Minister Ahmet Davutoğlu paid a number of visits to Damascus, the last of which took place on 9 August 2011, to persuade Syrian President Basher Assad to accept its mediation with the opposition in order to find a common ground in Syria. However, Turkey's attempts were rejected by Assad, who was convinced that he would win by force.[23] Subsequently, Turkey's initial neutral position in Syria shifted towards partial support of the Syrian opposition. As such, it was one of the initiators of the Friends of Syria Group, which was established in 2012 to exert pressure on the Syrian regime and support the opposition. Turkey hosted the second meeting of the group in Istanbul on 1 April 2012.

Turkey also hosted the United Nations High Commissioner for Refugees (UNHCR) meeting in Şanlıurfa on 17 January 2014 to discuss the situation of the Syrian refugees. It contributed to the processes of preparation and organization of the Geneva I and II meetings, and it is a member of the Syria Contact Group, which organizes the delivery of international aid into Syria, the majority of which passes through the Turkish border. Turkey has also absorbed almost 2 million Syrian refugees.

In Yemen, Turkey contributed to the establishment of the Friends of Yemen Group founded on 27 January 2010 and has been providing development and humanitarian aid to the country.[24] Turkey also supported the process of the National Dialogue Conference in Yemen, which was initiated by the Gulf Cooperation Council and carried out between 18 March 2013 and 24 January 2014 to ensure peaceful transition in Yemen.[25] During Erdoğan's visit to Iran in April 2015, he also proposed Iran as a co-mediator for the crisis in Yemen.[26] However, this option seems unlikely considering the level of hesitation toward Iran's mediator role in the country.

From Instituting Order to Preserving Areas of Influence

Turkey's mediation has been in the foreground of its foreign policy during the last decade or so as a result of a turn that has been informed by Turkey's response to certain international, regional and domestic developments. The end of the Cold War, the September 11 events, the Iraqi War, the Justice and Development Party (AKP)'s ascendance to power and the increasing level of prosperity in Turkey may be listed as some of the developments that triggered such a turn. Among these, particularly the Iraqi War was a catalyst for Turkish policymakers to revise their regional policy. As also put forward by Altunışık and Çuhadar, one of the consequences of the Iraqi War was that, 'the decline of traditional Arab powers, such as Egypt, left room for non-Arab countries like Turkey and Iran to fill in this regional vacuum'.[27] Tocci underpins in a similar vein that the regional vacuum and the unfolding disputes were significant in the emergence of Turkey's mediator role. She notes that, 'Turkey's efforts in mediating the manifold conflicts in the region can be credited partly to Foreign Minister Ahmet Davutoğlu's personal inclination, but mainly to the lack of effective mediation in the region'.[28]

As a result, Turkey appraised its advantages by repositioning itself as a peace and stability promoter and a soft power in neighbouring regions. It reconstructed its identity by referring to its historical–geographical depth in addition to its social and cultural affinities. Subsequently, Turkey has become more active in its neighbourhood and mediated in a number of peace talks, including the ones between Syria–Israel, Iran–the West, Croatia–Bosnia–Yugoslavia in the Balkans, the Sunni–Shia groups in Iraq, Somalia–Somaliland, Palestine–Israel and Georgia–Russia.

While its mediator role has been both praised and criticized among various circles, Turkish policymakers consider it as a means of bringing peace, stability and order to Turkey's areas of influence.[29] As such, mediation has been an instrument of realizing Turkey's regional policy, which was based on promoting high-level political dialogue through high-level strategic cooperation council agreements and regional cooperation mechanisms; developing economic interdependence through various trade agreements and the policy of lifting visas; building a comprehensive security framework; and promoting multicultural coexistence in the region through the inclusion of all actors. Turkey's mediator role was also coined as part of its much criticized 'zero-problems with neighbors' policy, which aimed to normalize relations and increase dialogue with neighbours through political, economic and social relations.[30] Mediation is also a tool of achieving foreign policy successes for the AKP that then enables it to sustain its status quo in domestic politics.

Turkey's mediation attempts delivered mixed results during the Arab Spring. While it was able to apply mediation in Bahrain, partially in Libya and in Iraq, its mediation attempts fell short of achieving any results in Syria and Yemen. For instance, in Libya, while its mediation to release the journalists delivered results, its mediation between the Gaddafi regime and the opposition failed as a result of the lack of a receptive audience. According to Altunışık, there will be limits to Turkey's soft power and mediation as long as the region continues to be under the influence of hard power.[31]

As also underpinned by Aras, 'Turkey's projection of its mediation role relies, to a large extent, on the assumption of itself being a credible actor and on the promotion of regional ownership and inclusiveness'.[32] For instance, Turkey's support for regional mechanisms, such as the Friends of Syria and Friends of Yemen initiatives, aims to resolve conflicts without taking too much risk by promoting regional ownership and burden sharing. Before the Arab Spring, Turkey's main assets as a mediator were its neutral and credible image, as well as its principle of 'all-inclusiveness' in its foreign policy. Although Assad initially rejected Turkey as a mediator because of his own ambitions and strong belief that he could win by force, Turkey has conspicuously sided with the opposition in Syria, as well as in other conflicts across the region such as in Egypt, Libya and Yemen, which has halted its neutral image as a mediator.

Until the Arab Spring, the main objective of Turkey's foreign policy was to expand from being a regional power to an international one. To be able to achieve that aim, Turkey tried to utilize mediation as an instrument of instituting order by ensuring stability and security in the region. However, the Arab Spring came as a surprise for policymakers and created a setback for Turkey's regional policy. As also contended by Öniş, it has also indicated the limits of Turkey's capabilities.[33] For instance, Turkey failed to predict the fall of the Gaddafi regime and the endurance of the Assad regime. Furthermore, the Libyan and the Syrian experiences demonstrated that Turkey cannot go too far against its Western allies, and it has limited independence as a regional player. Regardless of Turkey's ambitions to evolve into an international player, this seems rather difficult for an actor that is unable to maintain control even in its own backyard. As such, it may be argued that, during the Arab Spring, mediation turned from being a tool of instituting order to preserving Turkey's areas of influence. However, despite certain setbacks, mediation is still a relevant tool of foreign policy for Turkey.

Qatar as a Mediator during the Arab Spring[34]

Qatar mediated a number of talks during the Arab Spring. In September 2012, it mediated between the al-Nusra Front and the Fiji government for the release of 45 Fijian UN peacekeeping soldiers held captive by al-Nusra for two weeks. The soldiers were released following Qatar's mediation.[35] In March 2014, Qatar mediated the release of 13 Lebanese nuns kidnapped by militia groups in Maaloula in addition to the release of 9 Lebanese pilgrims after being detained for over a year in Aleppo.[36] In September 2014, Qatar also mediated between the Lebanese government, the Islamic State and al-Nusra over the release of 19 Lebanese soldiers and 20 policemen who had been abducted by two militia groups in August 2014.[37]

Qatar has been an active mediator in Yemen as well. Its mediator role in the country started back in 2007 between the Yemeni government and the Houthi rebels. Although Yemen's mediation proved fruitful and resulted in an agreement in 2008, the conflict re-erupted in 2009 as a result of Yemeni President Ali Abdullah Saleh's denouncement of the agreement. Another agreement was signed in 2010 but also failed to be implemented.[38] In February 2013, Qatar further mediated the release of a Swiss teacher in Yemen who had been abducted by tribesmen to be swapped in return for their jailed relatives.[39]

Al-Muslimi argues that during the Qatari-mediated talks between the Houthis and the Yemeni government back in 2009, Qatar sided with the Muslim Brotherhood affiliated Major-General Ali Mohsen al-Ahmar (who was also an advisor to the President and representative of the Yemeni government during the talks). When the revolutions began in Yemen in 2011, Qatar conspicuously sided with the opposition and publicly called on President Ali Abdullah Saleh to step down. It even funded the Yemen Youth Channel, a TV channel launched by the Muslim Brotherhood in Yemen.[40]

During the Arab Spring, Qatar also mediated between Hamas and Israel in July 2014. Its mediation came upon US request following the failure of Egyptian mediation, which was primarily due to Egypt's bias towards Hamas. Both the Egyptian government and Israel considered Hamas a terrorist organization. Egypt prepared the mediation agreement without even consulting with Hamas. As Hamas official Ezzat al-Rishq also underlined, Qatar was the only actor that developed communication with Hamas during the crisis. Qatar's neutrality was questioned during its mediation proposals between Hamas and Israel as well. Its role as mediator had come onto the table during the ceasefire talks during the Israel–Gaza crisis in 2014. Although US Secretary of State John Kerry was in favour of Qatar, its role was dismissed and, eventually, it was Egypt who brokered the ceasefire agreement. While Kerry regarded Qatar's close relations with Hamas as an asset, Israel was wary that Qatar might lean toward Hamas.[41]

From Ensuring Stability to Fostering Change

Qatar's mediator role has emerged in line with its new foreign policy adopted following former Emir Sheikh Hamad bin Khalifa Al-Thani's rise to power in 1995. Qatar has mediated a number of conflicts to date, including conflicts in Lebanon, Yemen, between Sudan and Darfur, Israel and Palestine, and recently in Syria.[42] Al-Thani envisioned Qatar as having a proactive foreign policy and playing an influential role in regional politics. Mediation was officially entered into the Qatari constitution in 2003 and subsequently adopted as a foreign policy imperative. The rise of Qatar as a giant energy exporter in the 1990s has also been influential in the carving of a more confident and active foreign policy.[43]

As contended by Ulrichsen, 'The shifting nature of the concept of power in an intensely interconnected world enabled small states such as Qatar to project far greater influence abroad.'[44] As a small state, Qatar's image as a peacemaker serves as a tool for ensuring its national security in a volatile region by reducing 'the number of regional or global opponents Qatar might face otherwise'.[45] In other words, mediation has been a tool of survival of the Qatari regime. As in the words of Ulrichsen, 'The most convincing explanation of Qatari regional and peace-making efforts lay in a multifaceted strategy of political and economic liberalization, state-branding, and pursuit of an independent foreign policy.'[46]

As a typical small state, Qatar benefited from stability in its region prior to the Arab Spring as it was important for its own regime security and used mediation as a tool of ensuring it. However, during the Arab Spring, Qatar's policy shifted from ensuring stability to fostering change as a result of the unpredicted regional developments. This was mainly due to the swift rise of Islamic groups in the region, particularly during the initial phase of the uprisings, raising expectations that they would become the future rulers. Qatar has long had close contacts with such groups, to the extent that it allegedly hosts prominent members of the Taliban, Hamas and the Muslim Brotherhood, as well as rebels from Syria and Libya.[47]

Another catalyst for change in Qatari foreign policy has been the beginning of the period of détente between the USA and Iran, which in turn agitated Saudi Arabia. As a result, Qatar has been able to move more freely in the region and fill in the vacuum created by decreased Saudi influence. Subsequently for Qatar, mediation has transformed into a tool for fostering change by intervening into the domestic politics in other countries. As such, the sudden twist in its foreign policy has revealed Qatar's ambitions to extend its influence, play a greater role and mould regional politics according to its interests. For instance, Qatar has become an active player in Yemeni politics to the extent that it challenged Saudi Arabia's long-standing sway in the country. As Ennis and Momani postulate, Qatar's 'competition as a regional mediator is pushing into traditionally Saudi diplomatic territory'.[48]

Qatar's promotion of change during the Arab Spring has been regarded by many circles as a demonstration of its ideological tendencies. It has been blamed for taking sides with the Islamists. In doing so, Qatar has been accused of utilizing its soft power through the use of its international media organ Al Jazeera. The channel was accused of supporting the Islamic rebels during the Arab Spring. For instance, three journalists from Al Jazeera were jailed in Egypt for supporting the Muslim Brotherhood during the protests. Similarly, Saudi Arabia, Bahrain and the United Arab Emirates also accused Al Jazeera of siding with the group.[49] Critics even suggest that the channel has turned into a propaganda tool rather than being an independent media outlet complying with the ethics of journalism.[50]

Being the country that has the highest GDP (gross domestic product) per capita among rentier states,[51] Qatar's massive financial resource as a mediator enables it to finance talks and implement peace agreements.[52] It has the financial ability to pay ransom money, as well as keep the promises it makes on the table.[53] During the Arab Spring, Qatar also utilized its financial capacity to foster change by supporting the oppositions. For instance, Qatar provided $400 million to the opposition in Libya, $3 billion in Syria and $5 billion in Egypt.[54]

Despite allegations that Qatar supported the Muslim Brotherhood during the Arab Spring, Qatari officials deny such claims. For instance, in an interview with *Al Hayat*, Qatari Foreign Minister Khalid al-Attiyah underpinned that Qatar does not support the Muslim Brotherhood. Regarding the initial phase of the Egyptian revolution, he notes that, 'We [Qatar] kept up our support without knowing who will rule next.

Then, Mohammed Morsi became president through the ballot box and we dealt with him as a president, not as a member of a party.'[55]

Until the Arab Spring, one of Qatar's main assets as a mediator had been its neutral and honest image as a peace-broker. Its position as a small state and lack of hard power enabled Qatar to foster such an image. The unfolding events of the Arab Spring came as a surprise to many countries in the region including Qatar and, subsequently, left them in a position to revise their existing foreign policies. The Arab Spring served as a venue for Qatar to test its neutral image as a mediator. As Barakat underpins, 'Qatar's foreign policy, meanwhile, shifted from a focus on patient mediation to one of advocating intervention and confrontation.'[56]

Another asset of Qatar as a mediator before the Arab Spring was its inclusive approach. Qatar's connections with several factions in the region provide it with an extensive network and flexibility as a mediator. However, during the Arab Spring, Qatari mediation has been somewhat more exclusive. For instance, Qatar refrained from informing or seeking the consent of the Yemeni authorities while mediating the release of the Swiss teacher abducted by al-Qaida.[57] Similarly, as outlined earlier in the text, Qatar was quick to exclude the governments of Libya, Egypt and Syria and side with the oppositions probably as a result of its early calculations and confidence toward a possible victory by the rebels.

During the Arab Spring, Qatar presented itself as an 'advocate of humanity'. It positioned itself on the side of the people uprising against their governments. For instance, regarding the release of the abducted Fiji soldiers, the Qatari Foreign Ministry maintained that its mediation 'came out of Qatar's belief in the principles of humanity' and 'Qatar will spare no effort to harness all its potential and diplomatic mechanisms to maintain life'.[58] For instance, Qatar has positioned itself on the side of the Syrian opposition during the civil war.[59] Its conflict resolution initiatives have included not only mediation but also advocacy and the promotion of the Syrian opposition on regional and international platforms. Qatar condemned and denunciated the Syrian regime following allegations that it had used chemical weapons in the Eastern Ghouta region of Damascus. It also called 'on the UN Security Council to issue a resolution for a ceasefire in Syria and find the mechanisms to implement it' and the Arab League 'to bear their responsibilities towards the Syrian people'.[60] In Libya as well, Qatar was quick to side with the opposition and provided it with large amounts of financial and military support.[61] However, while Qatar has advocated for the people in the Middle East on several platforms, it has also been criticized for violating human rights and exploiting foreign labour, signalling a mismatch between rhetoric and practice.[62]

In sum, it may be argued that before the Arab Spring, while Qatar used mediation as a tool for survival, during the Arab Spring it used mediation more as a tool of fostering change. For Qatar, the Arab Spring created a new opportunity. The centre of power in the Arab street has shifted towards the Gulf region as a result of the loss of power of traditional Arab actors such as Syria, Iraq and Egypt. While Saudi Arabia used to be the main player in the Gulf, its lack of operational abilities during the transition period from King Abdullah to King Salman ignited hopes and perhaps opportunity for Qatar to transition from small state to regional power.

Given its overall record during the Arab Spring, it is evident that Qatar was able to apply mediation as a tool of foreign policy and deliver results. Qatar met with a receptive audience as the conflicting parties, as well as other actors in the region, generally accepted its mediation. In conclusion, it can be argued that mediation was a relevant policy tool for Qatar during the Arab Spring.

Iran as a Mediator during the Arab Spring

During the Arab Spring, Iran offered to mediate in Iraq, Syria, Yemen and allegedly in Bahrain. All of these offers, however, were rejected. As a result, Iran has become known more for its rejected mediation rather than as a mediator per se. Iran's first mediation attempt in Iraq took place during the crisis between Vice-President Tariq al-Hashimi and Prime Minister Nouri al-Maliki that erupted in late 2011 as a result of the terrorism charges pressed against Hashimi. However, its mediation did not achieve any results since it was rejected by the Iraqiya faction because of the lack of trust in Iran's neutrality.[63] Iran's second mediation attempt in Iraq took place between the peshmerga and the Shia militia group Popular Mobilization Units (*Hashid Shaabi*) to join forces against the stronghold of the Islamic State in March 2015. Its mediation attempt was rejected during the first round of talks based on the claim that Iran leaned towards Popular Mobilization Units.[64]

In Syria, Iran offered to mediate between the regime and the opposition in September 2013. Its offer was rejected by the National Coalition, which claimed, 'The Iranian initiative is not serious and lacks political credibility', referring to Iran as 'part of the problem'.[65] Iran's close tie with the Assad regime in Syria is not a secret. In addition, Iran has strong ties with the Shia militia group Hezbollah, which has defended the Syrian regime throughout the uprisings. As a result, it is not a surprise that the Iranian proposal to mediate in Syria was perceived with scepticism on the part of the Syrian opposition.

Iran also allegedly attempted to mediate in Bahrain in May 2013. Regardless of Iranian allegations that Bahrain secretly asked Iran to mediate between the Bahraini government and the Shia opposition in the country, Bahraini Foreign Minister Shaikh Khalid Bin Ahmad Al Khalifa rejected such claims by arguing that, 'Bahrain has not and will not ask for a mediation in a domestic issue from anyone, least of all from Iran'.[66] During the crisis in Bahrain, both Bahrain and the Gulf Cooperation Council accused Iran of meddling in the domestic affairs of Bahrain. As such, Iran was perceived as a biased actor in Bahrain. Furthermore, it has been often regarded as a party to the conflict in the country, to the extent that several actors such as Turkey[67] and Algeria,[68] as well as allegedly the Gulf and Arab countries[69] and Oman,[70] offered mediation between Iran and Bahrain.

Iran's offer to mediate in Yemen in April 2015 was rejected by Yemeni Foreign Minister Riad Yassin on the grounds that 'Iran has become a major part of the Yemeni crisis and those who are a party to the crisis … cannot become mediators'.[71] Iran has been supportive of the Houthis in Yemen, a Shia group that, together with groups supportive of former Yemeni President Ali Abdullah Saleh, rebelled against the government of Abdrabbuh Mansour Hadi.[72]

From Expansionism to the Survival of the Regime

The Arab Spring was met with surging excitement in Iran, stimulating its expansionist ambitions towards the region. As also argued by Parsi, Iran 'had for quite some time expected and waited for the pro-American regimes in the region to fall. But they incorrectly predicted that those Islamist movements would view Tehran as a leader, as an ideological source.'[73] Parsi further notes that Iran was later on disappointed that the Islamic movements followed the ideological line of the Muslim Brotherhood or Wahabism rather than itself.[74] Jones contends similarly that, 'Over the course of the Arab Spring to date, we have witnessed emotions in Iran change from initial optimism, to growing concern, to outright worry.'[75] As such, the initial euphoric reaction of the regime in Iran, which referred to the Arab Spring as an 'Islamic Awakening' that would turn to Iran as an example, has been replaced with disappointment.[76]

Consequently, Iran's foreign policy priority during the Arab Spring has shifted from the implementation of an expansionist policy to one focused on the survival of its regime. What has characterized the Iranian foreign policy has been its fear of losing power in the region.[77] In order to ensure its survival, Iran has supported the Assad regime in Syria, as well as the Shia groups in Iraq, Bahrain and Yemen. Perhaps most importantly, it has tried to prevent the spill over of the revolutions into its own territory. In addition, the recent nuclear deal has marked a new era by ending the traditional enmity between the Iranian regime and the USA. As such, the centre of focus in Iran has shifted away from seeing the USA as the main threat to sectarianism.

In light of these developments, it may be argued that Iran used mediation for two main reasons. First, Iran used mediation as a tool of meddling into the domestic affairs of countries. Second, it used mediation as a protectionist and counter-revolutionary tool to secure its regional role. However, its mediation attempts failed to deliver any results since they had all been rejected. As evident in the above section, one of the main reasons for this failure was Iran's lack of credibility as an honest, neutral mediator. Furthermore, Iran has come to be known for the use of its hard power rather than soft power during the Arab Spring. As such, Iran clearly lacked legitimacy as a mediator since it was perceived rather as a party to the conflicts it aimed to mediate. Similarly, Iran lacked an audience that was receptive to its mediator role. In all of the mediations it offered, its role was made unwelcome by at least one of the conflicting parties. It was perceived as a biased, partial mediator. In conclusion, mediation has not been a relevant policy tool for Iran during the Arab Spring.

Conclusion

This paper aimed to understand to what extent mediation has been a relevant tool of foreign policy during the Arab Spring by examining the mediation attempts of Turkey, Qatar and Iran. To be able to answer that question, this study investigated why and how these actors mediated, to what extent they were able to apply mediation as a tool of foreign policy, whether their mediation attempts could deliver any results and whether there was a receptive audience with respect to their mediation.

While mediation stood out as a benchmark of Qatari foreign policy, mediation only played a partial role in Turkey's policy toward the Arab Spring. On the other hand, although Iran made a number of mediation attempts during the Arab Spring, these attempts were largely rejected. Each country's use of mediation has run parallel to the changes in its foreign policies during the Arab Spring. For instance, before the Arab Spring Turkey used mediation mainly as a tool of instituting order; during the Arab Spring it used mediation mainly as a tool of preserving its areas of influence. Similarly, Qatar's use of mediation has changed from a tool of ensuring stability to a tool of fostering change. Iran, on the other hand, used mediation as a tool of intervention that developed into a tool ensuring the survival of its regime. These examples validate the initial theoretical argument that when a mediator is a state, its use of mediation is in line with its foreign policy interests.

Among the three actors, Qatar was able to apply mediation in a number of hostage crises during the Arab Spring, all of which achieved results. The only case that did not achieve results was its mediation between Hamas and Israel. Turkey, on the other hand, achieved mixed results as a mediator. While its mediation echoed positive responses in Bahrain, it achieved partial results in Libya and Iraq. Furthermore, it was not able to achieve results in Syria and Yemen. Finally, Iran's mediation attempts did not achieve any results during the Arab Spring.

These examples also demonstrate an interesting finding that, during the Arab Spring, while mediation produced results in smaller conflicts such as hostage crises, it failed to achieve similar results in broader conflicts such as the ones between the regime and the opposition in Libya, Syria and Yemen. One of the reasons for such outcome may be that in broader conflicts the parties often have long-term objectives and anticipate that they might win by using force if they endure long enough. In hostage cases, however, the abductors often have short-term objectives and execute the operations for specific, instant gains. As such, they may be more prone to mediation attempts.

The neutrality of all three actors was questioned during the Arab Spring, which affected each country's legitimacy as a mediator. The fact that they all took sides raised criticism among some of the parties. As such, it is difficult to speak of a wide-scale receptive audience with respect to each country's mediation efforts. In addition, when mediators are partial they need to have enough power to support their positions. The inability of Turkey, Qatar and Iran to coerce parties into certain solutions during the Arab Spring also demonstrated the limits of their power capabilities.

In light of the above discussion, it may be argued that, during the Arab Spring, despite certain setbacks, mediation has nevertheless been a relevant policy tool. The unfolding events of the Arab Spring have once again proved the complexity of the region. Mediation, therefore, is an important tool of conflict resolution given the ineffectiveness of conventional ways in tackling conflicts. There is considerable potential for regional powers to take on mediator roles in these conflicts. However, the effectiveness of their mediation attempts depends, to a large extent, on their commitment and reliability as mediators.

Disclosure Statement

No potential conflict of interest was reported by the author.

Notes

[1] United Nations, *United Nations Guidance for Effective Mediation*, September 2012, <http://peacemaker.un.org/sites/peacemaker.un.org/files/GuidanceEffectiveMediation_UNDPA2012%28english%29_0.pdf> (accessed 15 March 2015).

[2] Josephine M. Zubek, Dean G. Pruitt, Robert S. Peirce, Neil B. McGillicuddy and Helena Syna, 'Disputant and mediator behaviors affecting short-term success in mediation', *Journal of Conflict Resolution*, 36(3), 1992, p. 546; Jacques Faget, 'The metamorphosis of peacemaking', in Jacques Faget (ed.), *Mediation in Political Conflicts: Soft Power or Counter Culture?*, Hart, Oxford, 2011, p. 3.

[3] Jacob Bercovitch, J. Theodore Anagnoson and Donnette L. Wille, 'Some conceptual issues and empirical trends in the study of successful mediation in international relations', *Journal of Peace Research*, 28(1), 1991, p. 8; Faget, op. cit., p. 3; Marieke Kleiboer, 'Understanding success and failure of international mediation', *Journal of Conflict Resolution*, 40(2), 1996, p. 360; James A. Wall, Jr., John B. Stark and Rhetta L. Standifer, 'Mediation: a current review and theory development', *The Journal of Conflict Resolution*, 45(3), 2001, pp. 370–391; I. William Zartman, *Negotiation and Conflict Management: Essays on Theory and Practice*, Routledge, Abingdon, 2008, p. 155.

[4] Oliver Ramsbotham, Tom Woodhouse and Hugh Miall, *Contemporary Conflict Resolution*, Polity Press, Cambridge, 2012, p. 184.

[5] Saadia Touval, 'Mediation and foreign policy', *International Studies Review*, 5(4), 2003, p. 91.

[6] Ibid., p. 91.

[7] James A. Wall, 'Mediation: an analysis, review, and proposed research', *The Journal of Conflict Resolution*, 25(1), 1981, p. 160.

[8] Mehran Kamrava, 'Mediation and Saudi foreign policy', *Orbis*, 57(1), 2013, p. 153.

[9] Mehran Kamrava, 'Mediation and Qatari foreign policy', *Middle East Journal*, 65(4), 2011, p. 540.

[10] Touval, op. cit., p. 92.

[11] Jacob Bercovitch and Richard Jackson, *Conflict Resolution in the Twenty-First Century: Principles, Methods, and Approaches*, University of Michigan Press, Ann Arbor, 2009, p. 38.

[12] 'Bahrain thanks Turkey over its role in ending turmoil', *Hurriyet Daily News*, 5 December 2011, <http://www.hurriyetdailynews.com/default.aspx?pageid=438&n = bahrain-thanks-turkey-over-its-role-in-diffusing-tension-2011-05-12 >; Patrick Goodenough, 'Turkey offers to mediate between Iran and Arab Gulf States over Bahrain crisis', CNSNews.com, 6 April 2011, <http://cnsnews.com/news/article/turkey-offers-mediate-between-iran-and-arab-gulf-states-over-bahrain-crisis>.

[13] Jeremy W. Peters, 'Freed *Times* journalists give account of captivity', *New York Times*, 21 March 2011, <http://www.nytimes.com/2011/03/22/world/africa/22times.html?_r=0 >.

[14] 'Turkey helps free *Guardian* journalist in Libya', *Hurriyet Daily News*, 17 March 2011, <http://www.hurriyetdailynews.com/turkey-helps-free-guardian-journalist-in-libya.aspx?pageID=438&n = -2011-03-17 >.

[15] Thomas Seibert, 'Turkey pursues its Libya mediation efforts despite setbacks', *The National*, 7 April 2011, <http://www.thenational.ae/news/world/europe/turkey-pursues-its-libya-mediation-efforts-despite-setbacks#full>.

[16] Ümit Enginsoy, 'Turkey a world apart on Libya sanctions', *Hurriyet Daily News*, 27 February 2011, <http://www.hurriyetdailynews.com/default.aspx?pageid=438&n=turkey-falls-apart-with-rest-of-world-on-libya-2011-02-27 >.

[17] Seumas Milne, 'Turkey offers to broker Libya ceasefire as rebels advance on Sirte', *The Guardian*, 27 March 2011, <http://www.theguardian.com/world/2011/mar/27/libya-turkey-mediators-prime-minister>.

[18] 'Libyan gov't to exclude Turkish companies from contracts', *Hurriyet Daily News*, 20 May 2015, <http://www.hurriyetdailynews.com/libyan-govt-to-exclude-turkish-companies-from-contracts-.aspx?pageID=238&nID = 78718&NewsCatID = 345 >.

[19] Emily O'Brien and Andrew Sinclair, 'The Libyan War: a diplomatic history—February–August 2011', New York University, Center on International Cooperation, New York, August 2011, p. 12.

[20] Seibert, op. cit.

[21] 'Turkey shuts down its embassy, revises Libya plans', *Hurriyet Daily News*, 2 May 2011.

[22] 'Chronology of foreign policy', *Turkish Foreign Ministry*, February 2011, <http://www.mfa.gov.tr/subat__.tr.mfa>.

[23] Nada Bakri, 'Turkish minister and other envoys press Syrian leader', *New York Times*, 9 August 2011, <http://www.nytimes.com/2011/08/10/world/middleeast/10syria.html?_r=0 >.

[24] 'The Fifth Ministerial Meeting of the Group of Friends of Yemen was held in London', *Turkish Foreign Ministry*, 7 March 2013, <http://www.mfa.gov.tr/the-fifth-ministerial-meeting-of-the-group-of-friends-of-yemen-was-held-in-london.en.mfa> (accessed 1 June 2015).

[25] '[S]upport for Yemeni National Dialogue Conference operations', *Turkish International Cooperation and Coordination Agency*, <http://www.tika.gov.tr/en/news/upport_for_yemeni_national_dialogue_conference_operations-8715> (accessed 7 June 2015).

[26] 'Turkey, Iran "should act together to stop bloodshed"', *Hurriyet Daily News*, 7 April 2015, <http://www.hurriyetdailynews.com/turkey-iran-should-act-together-to-stop-bloodshed.aspx?pageID=238&nID=80680&NewsCatID=510> (accessed 5 June 2015).

[27] Meliha Altunışık and Esra Çuhadar, 'Turkey's search for a third party role in Arab–Israeli conflicts', *Mediterranean Politics*, 15(3), 2010, p. 373.

[28] Nathalie Tocci, 'Foreword', in Nathalie Tocci, Ömer Taşpınar, Henri J. Barkey, Eduard Soler i Lecha and Hassan Nafaa (eds), *Turkey and the Arab Spring: Implications for Turkish Foreign Policy from a Transatlantic Perspective*, Mediterranean Paper Series, The German Marshall Fund, Institute Affari Internazionali, Washington, DC, October 2011, p. 4.

[29] Ahmet Davutoğlu, 'Turkey's mediation: critical reflections from the field', *Middle East Policy*, 20(1), 2013, p. 90.

[30] Ahmet Davutoğlu, 'Turkey's zero-problems foreign policy', *Foreign Policy*, 20 May 2010; Pınar Akpınar, 'Turkey's peacebuilding in Somalia: the limits of humanitarian diplomacy', *Turkish Studies*, 14(4), 2013, p. 740.

[31] Meliha Benli Altunışık, 'Challenges to Turkey's "soft power" in the Middle East', *TESEV*, June 2011, p. 2.

[32] Bülent Aras, 'Turkey's mediation and Friends of Mediation initiative', *Turkey Policy Brief Series*, Economic Policy Research Foundation of Turkey (TEPAV) and International Policy and Leadership Institute (IPLI), No. 6, 2012, p. 2.

[33] Ziya Öniş, 'Turkey and the Arab revolutions: boundaries of regional power influence in a turbulent Middle East', *Mediterranean Politics*, 19(2), 2014, pp. 211–212.

[34] This section has been reproduced from an earlier project on the Middle East and the Arab Spring (POMEAS) Policy Brief. See Pınar Akpınar, 'Qatar's regional aspirations: changing mediator role during the Arab Spring', *POMEAS Policy Brief*, No. 6, February 2015.

[35] 'Qatar's mediation helps free Fiji soldiers', *The Peninsula*, 12 September 2014, <http://thepeninsulaqatar.com/news/qatar/299785/qatar-s-mediation-helps-free-fiji-soldiers> (accessed 6 February 2015).

[36] Thomas El-Basha, 'ISIS "meets" Qatari mission over Lebanon hostages', *Al Arabiya*, 7 September 2014, <http://english.alarabiya.net/en/News/middle-east/2014/09/07/ISIS-meets-Qatari-mission-over-Lebanon-hostages-.html> (accessed 13 February 2015).

[37] 'Qatar's mediation helps free Fiji soldiers', op. cit.

[38] Kamrava, 'Mediation and Qatari foreign policy', op. cit., pp. 549–551.

[39] Mohammed Dabbous, 'Yemen kidnappers free Swiss woman after Qatari mediation: agency', *Reuters*, 28 February 2013, <http://www.reuters.com/article/2013/02/28/us-yemen-hostage-swiss-idUSBRE91R07J20130228> (accessed 21 February 2015).

[40] Farea Al-Muslimi, 'Qatar encroaches on Saudi influence in Yemen', *Al Monitor*, 20 August 2013, <http://www.al-monitor.com/pulse/tr/originals/2013/08/qatar-encroaches-saudi-influence-yemen.html> (accessed 20 February 2015).

[41] Amena Bakr, 'Qatar seeks role as Gaza mediator, Israel wary', *Reuters*, 17 July 2014, <http://www.reuters.com/article/2014/07/17/us-palestinians-israel-qatar-idUSKBN0FM2GD201 40717> (accessed 13 February 2015).

[42] Lina Khatib, 'Qatar's foreign policy: the limits of pragmatism', *International Affairs*, 89(2), 2013, p. 418; Kristian Coates Ulrichsen, 'Qatar's mediation initiatives', *NOREF Policy Brief*, February 2013, p. 1.

[43] Kristian Coates Ulrichsen, 'Qatar and the Arab Spring: policy drivers and regional implications', *Carnegie Endowment for International Peace*, 24 September 2014, p. 1.

[44] Ibid., p. 4.

[45] Kamrava, 'Mediation and Qatari foreign policy', op. cit., p. 542.

[46] Kristian Coates Ulrichsen, 'From mediation to interventionism', *Russia in Global Affairs*, 27 October 2013, <http://eng.globalaffairs.ru/number/From-Mediation-to-Interventionism-16170> (accessed 5 June 2015).

[47] David D. Kirkpatrick, 'Qatar's support of Islamists alienates allies near and far', *New York Times*, 7 September 2014, <http://www.nytimes.com/2014/09/08/world/middleeast/qatars-support-of-extremists-alienates-allies-near-and-far.html?_r=0> (accessed 19 February 2015).

[48] Crystal A. Ennis and Bessma Momani, 'Shaping the Middle East in the midst of the Arab uprisings: Turkish and Saudi foreign policy strategies', *Third World Quarterly*, 34(6), 2013, p. 1140.

[49] Amena Bakr, 'Defiant Al Jazeera faces conservative backlash after Arab Spring', *Reuters*, 2 July 2014, <http://www.reuters.com/article/2014/07/02/us-qatar-jazeera-media-idUSKBN0F70F120140702> (accessed 16 February 2015).

[50] Alexander Kühn, Christoph Reuter and Gregor Peter Schmitz, 'After the Arab Spring: Al-Jazeera losing battle for independence', *Spiegel Online International*, 15 February 2013, <http://www.spiegel.de/international/world/al-jazeera-criticized-for-lack-of-independence-after-arab-spring-a-883343.html> (accessed 17 February 2015).

[51] *CIA World Factbook*, 'Country comparison: GDP-per capita', 2012, <https://www.cia.gov/library/publications/the-world-factbook/rankorder/2004rank.html > (accessed 21 February 2015).

[52] Kamrava, 'Mediation and Qatari foreign policy', op. cit., p. 539.

[53] El-Basha, op. cit.

[54] Sultan Barakat, 'Qatari mediation: between ambition and achievement', *Brookings Doha Center Analysis Paper*, No. 12, 2014, p. 30.

[55] Khalid al-Attiyah, interview by *Al Hayat*, English translation by *Al Monitor*, 'Qatar Foreign Minister weighs means to protect Syrian people', 26 September 2013, <http://www.al-monitor.com/pulse/tr/politics/2013/09/qatar-foreign-minister-interview-syria-un.html#ixzz3Sa3ehCJa> (accessed 22 February 2015).

[56] Barakat, op. cit., p. 29.

[57] Farea al-Muslimi, 'Qatar encroaches on Saudi influence in Yemen', *Al Monitor*, 13 August 2014, <http://www.al-monitor.com/pulse/originals/2013/08/qatar-encroaches-saudi-influence-yemen.html#> (accessed 13 February 2015).

[58] 'Qatar's mediation helps free Fiji soldiers', op. cit.

[59] 'HE Foreign Minister meets head of Syrian Opposition Government', *State of Qatar, Ministry of Foreign Affairs*, 5 June 2014, <http://www.mofa.gov.qa/en/SiteServices/MediaCenter/News/Pages/News20140506212116.aspx> (accessed 7 February 2015).

[60] 'Qatar calls for Arab position supportive to any int. drive to halt Syria's extermination of its people', *State of Qatar, Ministry of Foreign Affairs*, 27 August 2013, <http://www.mofa.gov.qa/en/SiteServices/MediaCenter/News/Pages/News20130828091547.aspx> (accessed 7 February 2015).

[61] Barakat, op. cit., p. 30.

[62] 'Death toll among Qatar's 2022 World Cup workers revealed', *The Guardian*, 23 December 2014, <http://www.theguardian.com/world/2014/dec/23/qatar-nepal-workers-world-cup-2022-death-toll-doha> (accessed 13 February 2015).

[63] Alaa al-Lami, 'Iraqi factions row over Iranian mediation', *Al-Akhbar English*, 30 December 2011, <http://english.al-akhbar.com/node/2935>; Al Jazeera Centre for Studies, 'The Al-Hashimi crisis: position wars between the Iraqi forces', *Position Paper*, 16 January 2012.

[64] 'Iranian mediation between Peshmarga and Mobilization forces rejected, Kurdish sources', *Iraq Tradelink News Agency*, 20 March 2015, <http://www.iraqtradelinknews.com/2015/03/iranian-mediation-between-peshmarga-and.html>.

[65] 'Syria opposition rejects Iran mediation offer', *Al Jazeera*, 21 September 2013, <http://www.aljazeera.com/news/middleeast/2013/09/20139218174260390.html>.

[66] Habib Toumi, 'Bahrain denies Iran mediation request claim', *Gulf News Bahrain*, 8 May 2013, <http://gulfnews.com/news/gulf/bahrain/bahrain-denies-iran-mediation-request-claim-1.1180679>.

[67] Goodenough, op. cit.

[68] 'Algeria declares its readiness to mediate between Iran and Bahrain', *Middle East Monitor*, 2 April 2013, <https://www.middleeastmonitor.com/news/africa/5638-algeria-declares-its-readiness-to-mediate-between-iran-and-bahrain >.

[69] Habib Toumi, 'Bahrain dismisses reports on Arab mediation with Iran', *Gulf News Bahrain*, 8 April 2013, <http://gulfnews.com/news/gulf/bahrain/bahrain-dismisses-reports-on-arab-mediation-with-iran-1.1167880>.

[70] Habib Toumi, 'Oman denies Bahrain–Iran mediation drive', *Gulf News Bahrain*, 25 April 2013, <http://gulfnews.com/news/gulf/oman/oman-denies-bahrain-iran-mediation-drive-1.1175215>.

[71] 'Yemen FM rejects Iran mediation, insists rebels surrender', *The Daily Star*, 20 April 2015, <http://www.dailystar.com.lb/News/Middle-East/2015/Apr-20/295074-yemen-fm-rejects-iran-mediation-insists-rebels-surrender.ashx>.

[72] 'Yemen crisis: who is fighting whom?', *BBC*, 26 March 2015, <http://www.bbc.com/news/world-middle-east-29319423>.

[73] Trita Parsi, interview by Bülent Aras, *Project on the Middle East and the Arab Spring*, 29 August 2014, <http://www.pomeas.org/Home/index.php/interviews/447-interview-with-trita-parsi>.

[74] Ibid.

[75] Peter Jones, 'Hope and disappointment: Iran and the Arab Spring', *Survival*, 55(4), August–September 2013, pp. 73–84.

[76] 'Khamenei hails "Islamic" uprisings', *Al Jazeera*, 4 February 2011, <http://www.aljazeera.com/news/middleeast/2011/02/201124101233510493.html>.

[77] Jones, op. cit., p. 80.

Pınar Akpınar is a research fellow at the Conflict Resolution and Mediation stream of Istanbul Policy Center, Sabancı University. She is a PhD candidate at the School of Politics, International Relations and Philosophy, Keele University. Her research interests lie in the intersection between foreign policy and conflict resolution, with a particular focus on mediation and peacebuilding. She is also interested in the role of non-governmental organizations in peacebuilding and their impact on foreign policy.

Reform and Capacity Building in the Turkish Foreign Ministry: Bridging the Gap between Ideas and Institutions

Bülent Aras

Turkey has expanded the horizons of its foreign policy in geographical terms, as well as in terms of Ankara's involvement in global issues and in international organizations. Turkey's new foreign policy and line of geopolitical thought marks a considerable degree of discontinuity with the previous era. Turkey's ambition is to take on a central role in world politics under the guidance of the foreign policy vision of former Foreign Minister and current Prime Minister Ahmet Davutoğlu. This paper analyses the extent to which Turkey's Foreign Ministry has been able to transform itself in accordance with the new geopolitical thinking under Davutoğlu. It focuses on the capacity building and reform of the Foreign Ministry to understand how policymakers bridge the gap between ideas and institutions to ensure that the geopolitical perspective is an enduring and long-term project.

Introduction

Turkish foreign policy has developed a new geopolitical orientation that assumes Turkey will play an influential role in world politics. The interest in geopolitics among the policy community has been accompanied by a new academic awareness among Turkish students in this field. This scholarship is taking place at a time of change in Turkey, with its newly active and multidimensional aspects informed by geopolitical thinking based on a global outreach trajectory. A missing dimension in this emerging scholarship is the analysis of bureaucracy and institutions in foreign policymaking.

A framework of analysis evaluating the impact of novel rhetoric on institutions may help in understanding the extent to which bureaucracy adapts or resists new foreign policy thinking. It may also help to have an idea of the sustainability of the new geopolitical perspective. The successful transformation of the institutions depends on the ability of policymakers to enable and motivate the foreign policy apparatus to move forward in implementing new, tangible foreign policy.

This paper aims to analyse the extent to which Turkey's Foreign Ministry has been able to transform itself in accordance with the new geopolitical thinking. It will focus on Turkish geopolitics while emphasizing innovations in thinking about geography and the power within the foreign policy elite. A detailed discussion on Foreign Ministry reform and its connection with geopolitical thinking will be followed by an analysis of the gap between ideas and institutions in foreign policy. This analysis will conclude with an assessment of the sustainability of the new geopolitical thinking, with reference to the institutional adaptability to the changing framework of foreign policy.

Turkey's New Geopolitics

Turkey's new foreign policy and line of geopolitical thought marks a considerable degree of discontinuity with the previous era. The change in the policy is largely the result of the transformation of the domestic landscape, as well as the new regional and international environment. The new foreign policy framework of the ruling Justice and Development Party (JDP) played a constitutive role in the configuration of the new geopolitical thinking. The intellectual architect and practical implementer of this foreign policy is former Chief Advisor to the Prime Minister and Foreign Minister, current Prime Minister Ahmet Davutoğlu.[1]

The mindset of policymakers may change based on the impact of new situations both at home and abroad. The ideas, worldviews and imaginations of these political actors play a constitutive role in the description of the relationship between power and geography, and as a result, in the geopolitical thinking of policymakers.[2] The crux of the issue lies in establishing links between the changing domestic/regional environment and geopolitical thinking, and analysing how those ideas have been channelled into policy mechanisms and foreign policy practices. Davutoğlu is known for his influential book *Strategic Depth*, which calls into question how policymakers in post-Cold War Turkey misread the regional and international environment and thus failed to bring together the realities on the ground with Turkey's interests during this critical period.[3]

Davutoğlu's main contribution as foreign minister is his creation of a policymaking framework that sets up a balancing mechanism between domestic politics and foreign policy. The new context is less about geopolitical truths and constants as policymakers attempt to create a dynamic environment of inside/outside interaction for an operational geopolitical thinking. The domestic context is not free from domestic power struggles, but, nevertheless, it aims to liberate the geopolitical perspective from the limiting impact of domestic political contestations. The geopolitical thinking benefits from de-securitization at home and the expanding boundaries of normal politics.[4] In this way, it provides flexibility in foreign policy and helps remove barriers to open up the horizons of the geopolitical imaginations of policymakers.

Although the Foreign Ministry still enjoys its major role in policymaking, new state institutions like TİKA (providing development aid) and the Yunus Emre Foundation (promoting Turkish culture and language), along with Turks Abroad and Related Communities (dealing with Turkish Diaspora), have special responsibilities in foreign policy. There are also civilian actors who provide input into the policymaking process. In this plurality, Davutoğlu also undertook the task of coordinating those actors (as far as possible) and informing public opinion to mobilize support behind foreign policy.[5]

Although Davutoğlu's ideas in *Strategic Depth* constitute the cornerstones of his perspective, it would be unfair to consider this as the only guiding principle of the new geopolitical thinking. The new geopolitical thinking is a product of the formulation and practice of foreign policy in the ruling JDP era. It is still a work in progress. Turkey's geopolitical thinking is dynamic, subject to revision and influenced by the various changes in regional contexts, as well as other issues at stake.[6] Therefore, an analysis of Turkey's geopolitics requires focusing on its material and ideational sources and its dynamic nature in actual policy practice.

Central Country

Davutoğlu suggests the conceptualization of a 'central country' to encompass the qualities of the new geopolitical thinking for Turkey. According to him, a central country has undergone several historical transformations; been a cradle of grand political entities; is located at a cultural and economic intersection; and has influence in neighbouring countries and regions.[7] The central state gains meaning in an instrumental and functional sense. First, it is not something accorded simply due to geographical location. Location provides advantages if it is supported by strategic planning and power projection. Second, Turkey is identified as a potential central country as its geography is not much different from other central countries. Third, there is no emphasis on the notion that a weak state cannot survive in this geography. A weak state actually survived in the recent decades despite considerable problems and was the root cause of the country's passive situation in the region and beyond. Fourth, the new thinking demystifies geopolitics since it has more complicated and instrumentalist power assumptions in comparison to the classical school of geopolitics.

Geopolitical thinking assumes a powerful role for the Turkish state, as this thinking is a prerequisite for becoming a central power in world politics. The actual characteristics of this state and sources of its power are different from what is presented in the existing literature.[8] The focus in the literature is on the instrumentalist nature of the state, which only aims to serve the well-being of the citizens with the least possible ideological baggage. State mechanisms should be designed to reflect strong capabilities and a compassionate treatment that together would provide maximum benefit to the citizens.[9] This is a departure from earlier interpretations of the state as an organism as it also includes the state as an instrument with mechanisms and priorities.

The new power projection combines state capabilities and popular support to achieve Turkey's role as a central power in world politics. The instruments of power are strategic thinking, diplomatic skills, foreign policy bureaucracy, NGO (non-governmental organization) involvement, public diplomacy and economic activity.[10] The state mechanism benefits from the public's support since it is one of the major sources of power. The goal is to mobilize Turkish people behind policies in order to draw support and to provide legitimacy for the changing framework. The geopolitical openings were presented as an attempt to facilitate Turkish access to the new geographies, whether for humanitarian reasons, business or other purposes. As a result of this facilitation, among others, Turkish people 'pump blood to Anatolia'[11] through their investments or in preparation of the ground for further Turkish presence. In sum, although history and geography have provided advantages for Turkey to become a central country, this role should be solidified by a stable political atmosphere and economic development at home, as well as consolidation of Turkey's soft power in international relations.

Geographical Replacement

In terms of Turkey's geographic identity, Davutoğlu argues that Turkey has a well-established place in European history. Turkey's political, economic and social modernization have been guided by European-oriented ideas. He suggests a more dynamic and functional framework for relations with the European Union (EU), which will make Turkey a full member in due course and contribute to the EU's transformation into a global power.[12] Turkey's inclusion in the EU will empower the latter to consolidate its multicultural characteristic and provide access to Asia. He underlines that 'Turkey can generate new theses and find out solutions in the Eastern platforms with a confident claim of an oriental identity. It can discuss the future of Europe with its European perspective in the Western venues.'[13] The new geopolitics emerges from a self-confident attitude, considering itself European in historical and geographical terms, while having multiple regional identities at the same time. Without ignoring that this geography is a constitutive base of an ever-expanding geopolitical horizon, this perspective does not limit itself to the geography of cultural and historical affinities.

The tendency to prioritize regions in a way that may even create various conceptualizations of different geographies is no longer valid in the new thinking.[14] Geopolitical understanding is shaped around the idea that different regions are an integral part of a holistic vision. Davutoğlu underlines this difference with a new conceptualization of Turkish diplomacy. 'There is no constant line for diplomacy, but a platform of diplomacy. That platform is the whole world.'[15] The frontiers of geographic reach are global. The former distant geographies are no longer far away territories, and the new thinking accords Turkey a role and presence in global terms. The new mindset targets global diplomatic activity through an increasing number of diplomatic missions abroad. The continuous attempts to establish new embassies in geographies like Africa, Asia and Latin America are the result of this perspective. Policymakers see the fast-growing number of embassies and the increasing number of diplomatic personnel around the world as a sign of Turkey's gradual evolution into a central player in world politics.[16]

The second means of expanding geographic outreach is involvement in regional and global issues in order to provide Turkey with an international profile. Turkey's role in the issues of international importance would expand Turkey's virtual presence in the new geographies and consolidate its image as an influential player. Participation in international organizations with different capacities and leading roles in these platforms is part of this new notion. According to Davutoğlu, these attempts at different levels to elevate Turkey to a central position in world politics are complementary.[17]

The United Nations (UN) occupies a special place in the attempt to widen the country's geographic horizons. Turkey's non-permanent membership in the United Nations Security Council (UNSC) is central to this thinking and Turkish policymakers sought a new term after the 2008–10 period. The emphasis on the high number of votes for Turkey's UNSC membership supports Turkey's emerging central role in world politics.[18] The membership is also instrumental to enhancing Turkey's role in this direction. The UN provides a useful venue for disseminating Turkey's ideas and popularizing its foreign policy. Turkish policymakers claim Turkey's influence through policies on several issues and problem areas. For example, Turkey's leading role in the Friends of Mediation initiative highlights Turkey's perspective on conflict resolution and peacebuilding and aims to create awareness and guidelines in this realm within the UN system.[19] Turkey's leading role in the issues of least developed countries demonstrates another search for a role in the UN system; here Turkey is utilizing the absence of a major player. Turkey's active stance helps to justify and present its active policy, particularly in Africa, with a welcoming audience in the continent and on international platforms.[20]

Ideas and Institutions: Bridging the Gap through Capacity Building

A discussion on how ideas shape institutions requires a framework of causal links between policy changes and institutional adaptation. Policymakers see the translation of their political position into policy development as a major difficulty. However, the challenge is to structure institutions to enable them to appropriate the new policy choices as their future course of action. A consequential analysis from ideas to institutions in this framework would be helpful in this quest to understand how the Turkish Foreign Ministry is adapting itself to the new geopolitical thinking. However, both institutional and ideational approaches fail to address this problem, falling into characteristic traps that either simplify the role of ideas or amplify ideas for institution making.[21]

Turkish policymakers have developed two strategies for bridging the gap between new geopolitical thinking: the central country assumption and the foreign policymaking apparatus. These strategies include reform and redefinition of the roles in the Foreign Ministry and to create new institutions based on specific missions. One needs to look at how the Turkish Foreign Ministry faces the need for structural changes in order to adapt itself to the new ideational setting. The literature on the embedded institutions in bureaucratic mechanisms does not adequately explain this case. The focus is extensively on autonomy of the institutions.[22] The new structures in the Ministry do not have such autonomy and are not old enough for such an evaluation.

From a wider perspective, Turkey's new geopolitical thinking occurs in a process of social learning in a plural environment of state and civilian actors. Although the ideational entrepreneurs are present in this plural structure, the geopolitical thinking is mainly the product of policymakers as is the new architecture of the Ministry. The starting point for creating new mechanisms and structures within the Ministry is to prepare an institutional structure within the notion of a central country in world politics based on geopolitical thinking. As Moe argued, politicians like to structure institutions to make their ideas and influence as durable as possible.[23] Davutoğlu's persuasion played an important role in this process. He motivates other actors to move in the same direction to facilitate ideational and bureaucratic change in this plural environment. His active role in perpetuating and extending the geopolitical thinking found its expression in the Foreign Ministry reform.

The way in which bureaucracy responds to the introduction of new actors and organizational change is also relevant. Generally, they resist it. However, there may also be a receptive attitude, since bureaucrats may be concerned with losing their position or being unable to reap the benefits of new institutional opportunities.[24] There is a certain difficulty in assessing the resistance or willingness of reform and revision of the Foreign Ministry due to its thin and closed structure. In addition, officials do not reveal themselves in public. The evolution of the process and pace of adapting to the new environment may give some idea as to the reasons behind the bureaucratic response to structural change.

Rehabilitation of Human Resources

One crucial step in reforming the Ministry is restructuring the human resources system to make it functional, inclusive and active. The change in the structure of human resources was initiated with Law 6004.[25] The change was applied in the recruitment, education and working conditions of career diplomats. According to Ambassador Naci Koru, Deputy Foreign Minister, the idea is to make the necessary changes in human resources in order to facilitate personnel adaptation to fit the new scope and dynamism of Turkish foreign policy.[26]

A significant structural change to the old system is the classification of the personnel of the Ministry into two distinct groups: career diplomats and consular diplomats.[27] This new categorization aims to remove the psychological barrier between career diplomats and administrative personnel of the Ministry. It also seeks to motivate consular diplomats with a prospect of promotion to the rank of consul general and to encourage them to develop language skills. Career diplomats can also be promoted to the level of ambassador in a shorter period of time in comparison to the former arrangement.

As of February 2015, there are 2160 diplomats working at the Ministry.[28] Although there has been a steady increase in the number of diplomats recruited in the Ministry since 2000, the amount is still fairly modest compared to influential countries in international politics such as the USA (14,000), Germany, France (6000) and the UK. In that regard, the number of personnel recruited in the Ministry will be increased, aiming to reach a comparable level in 15 years' time.[29] After the new Law 6004, the Ministry started recruiting graduates from a wide variety of academic backgrounds, including law, history, sociology, psychology, economics and languages, as well as political science, international relations and public administration. Priority is given to those students proficient in foreign languages, in addition to their proven competency in the entry exam.

As a substantial investment in human resources, the Ministry encourages career diplomats to learn regional foreign languages to facilitate interaction with formal authorities and the local community during their posts abroad. The Human Resources Directorate General (İKAD) provides language-learning opportunities for career diplomats on a voluntary basis. It offers language courses in European languages (Spanish and Portuguese) and regional languages (Russian, Arabic, Persian, Serbian, Korean and Greek) at various levels. Law 6004 also encourages career diplomats to improve their academic capabilities by providing opportunities to obtain academic degrees in a specialization on specific regions or fields of study in international relations.[30]

Law 6004 improved working conditions such as employee benefits, easing the conditions of promotion, raising incentive allowances (in particular for new posts in African countries) and providing contributions to school expenses of the children of diplomats.[31] In addition, career diplomats have more flexibility to obtain posts at international organizations.[32] There are around 300 specialists who have been appointed from other public institutions to serve at Turkey's diplomatic missions abroad. The appointment of these temporary personnel is considered to be an important initiative for the opening of the personnel structure of the Ministry to other state institutions.[33] This compensates for the expertise deficit in the Ministry in the fields of law, trade, education and religious affairs, among others. Moreover, the new law permits appointment from other state institutions (namely, political appointments) to ambassadorial posts.[34] There are currently nine ambassadors, mainly from backgrounds in academia and other state institutions, appointed to posts. The number of such ambassadors is likely to increase in coming years.[35]

The Ministry of Foreign Affairs (MFA)'s special attention to the improvement of technical infrastructure to facilitate the efficient work of diplomats is also part of the restructuring process. According to Naci Koru, the Ministry has prioritized three areas in terms of technical infrastructure. First is the renovation and improvement of the information systems for representation abroad and work at home and renewal of all computers and electronic devices. The second is purchasing the necessary software systems and/or developing systems using the Ministry's own capabilities. The third is providing the necessary opportunities for the personnel to update and equip themselves for the efficient use of the information system.[36]

Koru also argues that while there has been an advanced information system used within the organization of the MFA, the pace of communication with the other ministries and institutions has not been satisfactory.[37] A project has been initiated to provide for electronic correspondence of the Ministry with other ministries, but this has not yet been completed. The improvements in the information systems of the representations abroad, the e-consulate system and the call centre for consular affairs have come to the fore as an important achievement in providing a better service to Turkish citizens living abroad. The *e-visa* system has also improved the provision of Turkish visas.

Institutional Reform within the Ministry

Much of the reorganization of the Ministry has been done in order to handle the increasing number and functions of Turkey's representations at international organizations and the new focus on issues of international importance. The number of the existing Directorate Generals of the Ministry has increased, mainly in the areas of international law, treaties, EU, global and humanitarian affairs, conflict prevention and crisis management, and bilateral political relations with neighbouring countries. The institutional capacity-building process of the Foreign Ministry can be analysed along two lines: the revision of the organizational structure of the Ministry and the creation of new bodies within the structure of the Ministry.

The increasing functions and responsibilities of a number of departments made it necessary to elevate already existing positions and ranking in the institutional structure of the Ministry. The Department of Information, Department of Protocol, Department of Policy Planning and Department of Intelligence and Research, formerly called 'departments', have been transformed into 'Directorate Generals'. Respectively, the new names are the *Directorate General for Information (ENGM)*, *Directorate General of Protocol (PRGM)*, *Directorate General for Policy Planning (SPGM)* and *Directorate General for Research and Security Affairs (AGGM)*.[38]

The organizational structure has been re-institutionalized at various levels. The number of Directorate Generals of the Ministry, which are the basic organization units for foreign policy planning and implementation, has increased from 15 to 25. In that regard, the recently established Directorate Generals are as follows: *Directorate General for International Law (UHGM)*, *Directorate General for Treaties (ANGM)* and two *Directorate General for Bilateral Political Affairs*, *Directorate General for Europe (AVGM)*, *Directorate General for Global and Humanitarian Affairs*, *Directorate General for Conflict Prevention and Crisis Management* and *Directorate General for Bilateral Economic Affairs (İEGM)*. The *Foreign Affairs Central Accountancy (DSAY)*, the *Directorate for Strategy Development (STGB)* and the *Directorate of Diplomatic Archives (DIAD)* are other recently established units concerning the need for better planning and implementation of Turkish foreign policy.

The newly constructed units are important elements for bridging the gap between the new geopolitical thinking in Turkish foreign policy and institutional capacity in the Ministry. However, as a senior diplomat underlined, some of the newly established units are currently not active due to the lack of qualified personnel.[39] For instance, considering the newly established *UHGM* and *ANGM*, although the Director Generals are appointed for these new bodies, the lack of qualified personnel with expertise and experience in municipal law and international law undermines the creation of these units. Similarly, the newly established Directorate General for Conflict Prevention and Crisis Management is not operational, and, in practice, the related activities are carried out under the *SPGM*.

Turkey's search for a more influential role through renewed attention and presence in international organizations also requires the creation of new structures and strengthening of existing departments. Turkey has increased its presence and weight in international organizations to foster its global presence and role in world politics.

The primary strategy is to become involved in a wide range of issues such as environment, climate change, population mobility, gender, cultural affairs, development, human trafficking, drugs and crime, disarmament, energy, terrorism, etc. Turkey has also increased the number and position of the diplomats working in the various departments and commissions in relevant international organizations.

Turkish foreign policymakers have prioritized working on various commissions, councils and sub-organizations of the UN. One example is Turkey's involvement in the 'Global Initiative to Combat Nuclear Terrorism' (GICNT) since 2006. In addition, Turkey was one of the 47 countries that participated in the Nuclear Security Summit (Washington, DC, 12−13 April 2010), which was aimed at developing a common understanding of strengthening nuclear security and reducing the threat of nuclear terrorism. The leading roles in the UN platforms like Friends of Mediation or Least Developed Countries (LDCs) and UN Humanitarian Summit are part of this new notion.

Partaking in these initiatives and activities facilitated by the UN, Turkey announced its candidacy for a non-permanent seat on the UNSC for the 2015−16 period. In order to promote its candidacy, Turkey initiated formal and informal dialogue mechanisms for lobbying in various countries around the world. In addition to the traditional diplomatic ties carried out by the Ministry's outside representation, informal contacts acted as an important means of gaining the support of various countries. The most important actors engaged in informal dialogues are special representatives. In that respect, Turkish ambassadors appointed as special national representatives paid visits to several countries to get their support for Turkey's candidacy to the non-permanent seat at the UNSC.[40]

At the regional level, Turkey's involvement focuses mainly in the political and economic spheres. Turkey is represented in the West African States Economic Community (ECOWAS), Eurasia Economic Community, East and South Africa Common Market (COMESA), South Africa Development Community (SADC), Economic Cooperation Organization (ECO) and Southern Common Market (MERCOSUR). Turkey has also initiated high-level cooperation councils with Central Asian, Balkan and Middle Eastern countries to facilitate regional integration.

In line with Turkey's policy of opening up to new geographies, Ankara has deepened its relations with the African Union (AU), the Association of Southeast Asia Nations (ASEAN), the East Africa Community (EAC), Organization of South Asia Regional Cooperation (SARC), Gulf Cooperation Council (GCC), Arab League (AL), Organization of Islamic Cooperation (OIC) and Association of Caribbean States (ACS-AEC). Turkey recently gained the status of dialogue partner for political cooperation in the Shanghai Cooperation Organization (SCO) in 2012.

Considering the aforementioned physical and thematic expansion of Turkey's representations in regional and international organizations, Turkish diplomacy has encountered a considerable increase in workload regarding the organization of joint cabinet meetings, hosting presidencies, organizing conferences and events, etc. Turkey also plays a key role in the conclusion of fundamental documents and agreements that guide the proceedings of concerned international organizations. The upcoming major international conferences in Turkey over the next few years—including the UN Least Developed Countries Summit (2015), the UN Humanitarian Summit (2016), the Organization of Islamic Cooperation Summit (2016) and the World Oil Congress (2017)—attest to the breadth of rhythmic diplomacy and global activism. This dynamic environment of multinational interaction mechanisms and initiatives necessitates a structural capacity building both in national missions abroad and relevant departments in Ankara dealing with these issues.

Three director generals and their related deputy director generals are responsible for issues concerning international organizations, namely, the Directorate General for International Security Affairs (NATO (North Atlantic Treaty Organization), OSCE (Organization for Security and Co-operation in Europe), Arms Control and Disarmament) (UGGM), Directorate General for Multilateral Political Affairs (International Political Organizations, Council of Europe and Human Rights) (ÇSGM) and Directorate General for Multilateral Economic Affairs (ÇEGM). Among these structures, there has been coordination and cooperation among the respective deputy director generals in the related thematic areas of international organizations. In this regard, the UGGM plans and coordinates the activities and policies in its area of responsibility through two deputy director generals, one specifically dealing with the issues related with OSCE, Arms Control and Disarmament, and the other with NATO and Euro-Atlantic Security and Defense Affairs.

The ÇSGM, the main unit in the organizational structure of the Ministry dealing with international political institutions, plans and designs its activities with two deputy director generals. One deals with matters of the Council of Europe and Human Rights while the other works with international political organizations, specifically the UN. The ÇEGM undertakes a major role in dealing with international organizations for economic affairs. In that regard, the Deputy Directorate General for Multilateral Economic Affairs (ÇEGY) deals with the basic international organizations for economic affairs such as the OECD and the G-20 process. The Deputy Directorate General for Energy, Water and Environmental Affairs (ESGY) is responsible for the related thematic issues under the UN framework. In addition to them, the Deputy Directorate General for Immigration, Asylum and Visa Affairs (KGGY) deals with international organizations in its related area of responsibility.

There is no newly established directorate general for specific international organizations under Law 6004. As some of the new units are currently not active, reorganization of the existing directorate generals is vital for the practical extension of coverage of Turkish foreign policy. The increasing number of personnel recruitment provides some relief.

Geographic Reorientation

The expanding horizons of Turkey's foreign policy and its new geopolitical focus are demonstrated by the increasing pace at which new missions in geographies of interest are being opened, for instance, in Africa, Asia and Latin America. This move has been accompanied by the deployment of new consulate generals to widen the scope of activity in countries that are already represented. The capacity of older missions is also being increased.

Davutoğlu sees the embassies as the main engines behind Turkey's official and civilian activities all over the world. He expects the personnel in the new missions to adopt a multi-track style of diplomacy. They will be dealing with the economy, education and culture, in addition to their usual diplomatic duties and responsibilities.[41] The Ministry's rapid response to the leadership's desire to reach out to new geographies indicates a positive and efficient strategy in line with the new foreign policy vision. One reason for the receptive attitude among the Ministry's bureaucracy is the increasing number of high-level posts that have been made available. However, the increasing number of personnel does reduce the chance of ending up as an ambassador. Some of these new missions will operate in the newly opened geographies and work with a limited number of personnel. As one senior Ministry official indicated, the adaptability of the Ministry to the new geographic scope of foreign policy is to a considerable extent their approval of the new foreign policy vision despite these difficulties.[42]

Although it is a traditional part of diplomacy, opening new embassies and representations is no easy task. Deputy Minister Naci Koru has underlined the difficulty and laborious process of opening embassies and missions abroad. He also pointed out that there is almost no country comparable to Turkey in terms of the pace at which it is opening new embassies in the world.[43] Turkey is seventh in terms of representation abroad and aims to move up. There are 228 missions all over the world, consisting of 134 embassies, 81 consulate generals, 12 permanent representatives and 1 trade office. The rise in the number of missions abroad has followed an interesting pattern since 2000, when there were 92 embassies and 160 representations abroad. This number increased to 99 embassies and 178 missions in total in 2009, and since 2009, these numbers have increased to 129 and 219, respectively.[44] The geographic expansion of the Turkish missions abroad has mainly occurred under the leadership of Davutoğlu, who became foreign minister in 2009. Davutoğlu has been able to mobilize the Ministry in catching up with the new foreign policy thinking largely through this ambitious move to open new missions at an unprecedented pace and scale. He was also able to generate support from the administration to finance and back Turkey's increasing representation all over the world.

The institutional adaptation process is about harmony and interaction among the Ministry's personnel abroad and in Turkey. In order to promote such a relationship, the Foreign Ministry organizes an annual ambassadors' meeting called the *Ambassadors' Conference* to ensure that the increasing number of ambassadors abroad are on board with the foreign policy thinking and practice. Launched in 2008, the *Ambassadors' Conference* is designed to act as a platform for information and consultation.[45] The conferences are organized in different cities in Turkey, gathering all ambassadors abroad and at home for the purpose of evaluating the previous year and discussing future prospects for Turkish foreign policy. The ambassadors meet with the foreign minister, other ministers and high-level bureaucrats and participate in internal evaluation meetings in the Ministry to discuss various regional and thematic aspects of foreign policy. In addition to this conference, there are also issue-specific and region-oriented meetings with related ambassadors. For example, there were specific gatherings of the ambassadors of Africa, Asia, and Middle East and North Africa in 2013. These meetings aim to coordinate policies and establish a mutual feedback mechanism between Ankara and the ambassadors abroad. Ambassadors also have the opportunity to bring their issues to the Ministry's agenda and to reach out directly to high-level Ministry officials.

Conclusion

An analysis of the dynamic interaction of ideas and institutions in foreign policy is a timely endeavour; however, it is necessary to undertake this in order to understand the link between the new rhetoric of foreign policy and reform in the MFA. The aim of this discussion is to analyse the change in the Foreign Ministry within the context of the new geopolitical thinking and to understand the extent to which the institutions are in line with Davutoğlu's foreign policy positions. Turkey has developed a new and instrumentalist geopolitical thinking with an ever-expanding thematic and geographic focus. It aims to project its power and seeks a central role in world politics. The new framework requires capacity building, recalibration and restructuring of the foreign policymaking apparatus. The analysis is limited to the capacity building and reform of the Foreign Ministry in order to understand how policymakers bridge the gap between ideas and institutions to ensure that the geopolitical perspective is an enduring and long-term project. This discussion also sheds light on the applicability and sustainability of the new geopolitical perspective.

The Ministry's reform aims to provide the necessary infrastructure and improve human capital within the Ministry to meet the capacity-building requirement vis-à-vis the expanding geographic and thematic focus of the new foreign policy. According to Davutoğlu, the Ministry is a source of power for the implementation of the new geopolitical perspective in distant territories and a wide range of international institutions.[46] The new Law 6004 and internal restructuring of the Ministry have provided the basis for change and improvement across a wide range of areas. At the top of this reform, there remains the decisive political will to change the institutional structure in a way that facilitates the implementation of a new geopolitical perspective.

There are considerable changes taking place in terms of the improvement of working conditions both at home and in newly opened embassies abroad, such as incentives to work in difficult geographies, including support for child education, increasing number of personnel and encouraging work in international institutions. In addition, Law 6004 increased the number of directorate generals in specific areas, mainly to account for the personnel working in newly opened geographies and on thematic issues of international importance. The ever-increasing number of embassies, consulate generals and representations at international organizations placed Turkey seventh internationally in terms of number of missions abroad.[47]

The Ministry has demonstrated a considerable degree of adaptability to the change required by the new geopolitical vision. The reforms improved the working conditions for Ministry personnel; new missions increased the chance of early appointment to ambassadorial posts and empowered diplomats in their dealings with counterparts. However, the new framework of foreign policy substantially increased workload, duties and responsibilities both at home and in missions abroad. Although there is support for the new geopolitical vision, as one senior diplomat indicated, there is also scepticism about the sustainability of opening up to new geographies.[48]

The new embassies operate with a limited number of personnel and are not necessarily diplomats' first choice for postings. The number of personnel is the highest it has ever been, and there seems to be a will to continue in this direction. However, the departments in the Ministry still suffer from a lack of personnel and, thus, a heavy workload. Another challenging task that lies ahead is the recruitment and training of personnel with the necessary professional, language and intellectual skills. Despite considerable progress, the demand for personnel with specific skills far exceeds existing capacity. Further work and capacity building is necessary.

The new directorate generals established by Law 6004 for specific issues are not operational; thus, the associated duties are shared by other directorates. For example, the Directorate General for Conflict Management and Mediation is not operational, and the related issues are handled by the Policy Planning Unit. The directorate generals of treaties and international law only exist on paper. There are not any new directorates for international organizations. As discussed, the responsibility for the new initiatives in the UN, changing the status of representation in and new relations with the international institutions is distributed among a limited number of departments. One deputy director general is responsible for almost all of them. Ertuğrul Apakan, former permanent representative to Turkey's mission at the UN, points out Turkey's permanent mission at the UN was supported with additional personnel during its non-permanent membership at the UNSC and Turkey's activism in this tenure is mostly handled through this channel.[49]

The Ministry's ability to generate support for increasing the number of missions abroad to 221 in such a short period of time is a considerable achievement. The pace of this opening up in new geographies is a remarkable response to the global scope of the new geopolitical thinking. The Ministry's internal restructuring is a necessary response to the issues pertaining to the newly established embassies and other missions all around the world. However, the division of labour in the Ministry has not changed to reflect the widening geographic focus. The deputy undersecretaries and director generals under them are responsible for the entire operation of these newly opened missions. In this sense, one director general, three deputy director generals and five heads of department as senior personnel in their units deal with 18 countries in the Middle East. Additionally, one director general, one deputy director general and four heads of department as senior personnel deal with 35 countries in Africa. Despite the ambitious rhetoric, only one small department deals with Turkey's Africa openings and all the complications and difficulties that go along with this. The situation is no different concerning Latin America and Asia. If the new geopolitical orientation of Turkey is going to operate as such, then it must consider these new openings vital to Turkey's future role in world politics and staff these missions accordingly.

Turkey has expanded the horizons of its foreign policy not only in geographical terms but also in terms of Ankara's involvement in global issues and in international organizations. Turkey's ambition is to take on a central role in world politics. Indeed, what is largely different about this new geopolitical perspective from the old is the development of Turkey's instrumental dimension, alternative power projection and new ties with international organizations. There has been considerable progress on this front, with positive signs that the Ministry is receptive to adapting itself to a new policy framework. However, as this discussion has demonstrated, there remains a gap between ideas and institutions, notably with regard to division of labour and resources needed to handle the new policy framework.

The current reforms mark the first wave of institutional adaptation and capacity building, setting up the infrastructure for the new missions abroad, Turkish presence on international platforms, dealing with new issues, and improving working conditions and professional training of diplomats. There is still need for restructuring and capacity building for the new directorate generals, for expanding the infrastructure to support the new policy framework, for recruiting and training diplomats for the new geographies and issue areas, and for developing the capacity to fine tune and recalibrate foreign policy goals. Despite the need for further capacity building to bridge the gap between ideational framework and the Foreign Ministry infrastructure, the progress in terms of institutional adaptability to new geopolitics is exemplary. There are strong grounds for arguing that Turkey's new geopolitics has found a receptive audience in the foreign policy bureaucracy. This readiness to undertake future challenges augurs well for the sustainability of the new policy.

Disclosure Statement

No potential conflict of interest was reported by the author.

Notes

[1] B. Aras, 'Davutoğlu era in Turkish foreign policy revisited', *Journal of Balkan and Near Eastern Studies*, 16(4), 2014, pp. 404–418.

[2] See J. A. Agnew, *Geopolitics: Revisioning World Politics*, Routledge, London, 1998; S. Dalby and G. Ó. Tuathail, 'The critical geopolitics constellation: problematizing fusions of geographical knowledge and power', *Political Geography*, 15(6–7), 1996, pp. 451–456; G. Ó. Tuathail, *Critical Geopolitics*, University of Minnesota, Minnesota, 1996; G. Ó. Tuathail, *Rethinking Geopolitics*, Routledge, London, 1998; G. Ó. Tuathail, 'Geopolitical structures and geopolitical cultures: towards conceptual clarity in the critical study of geopolitics', in Lasha Tchantouridze (ed.), *Geopolitics: Global Problems and Regional Concerns*, Centre for Defence and Security Studies, Winnipeg, 2003.

[3] A. Davutoğlu, *Stratejik Derinlik: Türkiye'nin Uluslararası Konumu* [*Strategic Depth: Turkey's International Position*], Küre, İstanbul, 1999.

[4] A. Balcı and T. Kardaş, 'The changing dynamics of Turkey's relations with Israel: an analysis of securitization', *Insight Turkey*, 14(2), 2012, pp. 99–120.

[5] Aras, op. cit.

[6] M. Yeşiltaş, 'The transformation of the geopolitical vision in Turkish foreign policy', *Turkish Studies*, 14(4), 2013, pp. 661–687.

[7] A. Davutoğlu, *Teoriden Pratiğe. Türk Dış Politikası Üzerine Konuşmalar* [*From Theory to Practice. Speeches on Turkish Foreign Policy*], Küre, İstanbul, 2013.

[8] See P. Bilgin, '"Only strong states can survive in Turkey's geography": the uses of "geopolitical truths" in Turkey', *Political Geography*, 46(7), 2007, pp. 740–756.

[9] A. Davutoğlu, 'Turkey's humanitarian diplomacy: objectives, challenges and prospects', *Nationalities Papers: The Journal of Nationalism and Ethnicity*, 41(6), 2013, p. 866.

[10] Ibid., p. 870.

[11] Ibid., p. 867.

[12] A. Davutoğlu, 'Turkish foreign policy and the EU in 2010', *Turkish Policy Quarterly*, 8(3), 2009, p. 15.

[13] Foreign Minister Ahmet Davutoğlu's speech at the 5th Annual Ambassadors' Conference in Ankara, 2 January 2013, <http://www.mfa.gov.tr/disisleri-bakani-sayin-ahmet-davutoglu_nun-v_-buyukelciler-konferansinda-yaptigi-konusma_-2-ocak-2013_-ankara.tr.mfa> (accessed 21 May 2015).

[14] E. Erşen, 'The evolution of "Eurasia" as a geopolitical concept in post-Cold War Turkey', *Geopolitics*, 18(1), 2013, pp. 24–44.

[15] 'Davutoğlu: Hattı Diplomasi Yoktur Sathı Diploması Vardır, Satıh ise Tüm Dünyadır' [There is no constant line for diplomacy, but a platform of diplomacy. That platform is the whole world], *Radikal*, 5 January 2010, <http://www.radikal.com.tr/politika/davutoglu_hatti_diplomasi_yoktur_sathi_diplomasi_vardir_satih_ise_tum_dunyadir-972801> (accessed 21 May 2015).

[16] Interview by the author with İbrahim Kalın, Deputy Undersecretary of Prime Ministry and Chief Advisor to Prime Minister, Ankara, 13 February 2014.

[17] A. Davutoğlu, 'Turkey's foreign policy vision', *Insight Turkey*, 10(1), 2008, pp. 77–96.

[18] B. Aral, 'Turkey in the UN Security Council: its election and performance', *Insight Turkey*, 11(4), 2009, pp. 151–168.

[19] B. Aras, 'Turkey's mediation and Friends of Mediation initiative', *SAM Papers*, 1(4), 2012.

[20] P. Akpınar, 'Turkey's peacebuilding in Somalia: the limits of humanitarian diplomacy', *Turkish Studies*, 14(4), 2013, pp. 735–757.

[21] M. Blyth, 'Structures do not come with an instruction sheet: interests, ideas and progress in political science', *Perspectives on Politics*, 1(4), 2003, p. 699.

[22] T. M. Moe, 'The politics of bureaucratic structure', in J. E. Chubb and P. E. Peterson (eds), *Can the Government Govern?*, The Brookings Institution, Washington, DC, 1989, pp. 267–329.

[23] Ibid.

[24] Blyth, op. cit., p. 699.

[25] Dışişleri Bakanlığının Kuruluş ve Görevleri Hakkında Kanun [Law on Establishment and Duties of the Ministry of Foreign Affairs of the Republic of Turkey]. For full text, see <http://www.mfa.gov.tr/data/BAKANLIK/mevzuat-2013.pdf> (accessed 21 May 2015).

[26] Interview by the author with Ambassador Naci Koru, Deputy Foreign Minister, Ankara, 22 August 2013.

[27] See Article 10, Paragraphs 1 and 2 of Law 6004.

[28] These figures were obtained from the Public Diplomacy Office in Prime Ministry, 7 May 2015, <http://kdk.gov.tr/sayilarla/13-yilda-65-yeni-temsilcilik-turkiyenin-yurtdisindaki-temsilcilik-sayisi-228e-cikti/41> (accessed 21 May 2015).

[29] Davutoğlu's speech at the 5th Annual Ambassadors' Conference, op. cit.

[30] See Article 19, Paragraph 1 of Law 6004. In 2013 and 2014, 28 diplomats pursued MA studies abroad, 12 diplomats studied at special MA programmes in Turkish universities with combined language programmes in countries of interest, <http://kdk.gov.tr/sayilarla/13-

yilda-65-yeni-temsilcilik-turkiyenin-yurtdisindaki-temsilcilik-sayisi-228e-cikti/41>
(accessed 21 May 2015).

[31] See Articles 16 and 17 of Law 6004.

[32] There are 17 diplomats working at various international organizations such as NATO, UN, BSEC (Black Sea Economic Cooperation), UNESCO, etc.

[33] For example, in 2012, the Ministry of Justice started to send experienced personnel as attachés to posts that required support and advice in legal affairs.

[34] See Article 12, Paragraph 2 (d) of Law 6004.

[35] Interview by the author with a senior diplomat, Ankara, 7 April 2014.

[36] Interview by the author with Ambassador Naci Koru, Deputy Foreign Minister, Ankara, 22 August 2013.

[37] '5. Büyükelçiler Konferansı' [5th Annual Ambassadors' Conference], *SonDakika.com*, 2 January 2013, <http://www.sondakika.com/haber/haber-5-buyukelciler-konferansi-4216939/> (accessed 21 May 2015).

[38] For the new arrangement of these departments, respectively, see Article 12, Paragraph 2 (d) of Law 6004; Article 6, Paragraph 2 (l) of Law 6004; Article 6, Paragraph 2 (n) of Law 6004; Article 6, Paragraph 2 (a) of Law 6004; Article 6, Paragraph 2 (k) of Law 6004.

[39] Interview by the author with a senior diplomat, Ankara, 6 May 2013.

[40] Ambassador Atılay Ersan's visit to the countries in the Pacific islands such as Nauru, Fiji, Vanuatu and Kiribati in 2012 exemplify Turkey's recent approach of promoting its candidacy to the UNSC for the period 2015–16.

[41] Foreign Minister Ahmet Davutoğlu's speech at 4th Annual Ambassadors' Conference in Ankara, 23 December 2011, <http://www.mfa.gov.tr/disisleri-bakani-sn_-ahmet-davutoglu_nun-iv_-buyukelciler-konferansi-acis-konusmasi_-23-aralik-2011.tr.mfa> (accessed 19 June 2014).

[42] Interview by the author with a senior diplomat, Ankara, 6 May 2013.

[43] Interview by the author with Ambassador Naci Koru, Deputy Foreign Minister, Ankara, 22 August 2013.

[44] These figures were obtained from Public Diplomacy Office in Prime Ministry, 7 May 2015, <http://kdk.gov.tr/sayilarla/13-yilda-65-yeni-temsilcilik-turkiyenin-yurtdisindaki-temsilcilik-sayisi-228e-cikti/41> (accessed 21 May 2015).

[45] For example, the 5th Annual Ambassadors' Conference was held with the theme of 'humanitarian diplomacy' in Ankara and Izmir on 2–7 January 2013. The final declaration of the conference reiterates that Turkish foreign policy will continue to be carried out with a multidimensional, visionary and self-confident approach to active foreign policy. The conference took place with a broad base of participation at the highest level including the President, the Prime Minister, the Foreign Minister, several members of the cabinet, as well as the foreign ministers of Singapore, Brazil and Sweden as foreign guest speakers of the conference.

[46] Davutoğlu, 'Turkey's humanitarian diplomacy', op. cit., pp. 865–870.

[47] See Office of Public Diplomacy at <http://www.kdk.gov.tr/sayilarla/10-yilda-58-yeni-temsilcilik/41> (accessed 21 May 2015).

[48] Interview by the author with a senior diplomat, Ankara, 7 April 2014.

[49] Interview by the author with Ertuğrul Apakan, former Undersecretary of Foreign Ministry and Permanent Representative to the United Nations, Istanbul, 24 October 2013.

Bülent Aras is Senior Scholar and Coordinator of the Conflict Resolution and Mediation stream at Istanbul Policy Center, Professor of International Relations in the Faculty of Arts and Social Sciences at Sabancı University and Global Fellow at Wilson Center. He is the Academic Coordinator of POMEAS (Project on the Middle

East and Arab Spring). His current research interests include geopolitics of the Arab Spring, non-state actors in peacebuilding, and bridging the gap between theory and practice in foreign policy. Recent work has been published in *Third World Quarterly*, *Middle East Policy*, *International Peacekeeping*, *Political Science Quarterly*, *International Journal*, *Journal of Balkan and Near Eastern Studies* and *Journal of Third World Studies*.

Practical Geopolitical Reasoning in the Turkish and Qatari Foreign Policy on the Arab Spring

Özgür Pala and Bülent Aras

As a regional power, Turkey aspires to become an influential international actor. As a small state, Qatar seeks to enhance its security and sovereignty and become an indispensable regional middle power. The Arab Spring protests have created an ideal context for both actors to realize their geopolitical goals. However, adverse political developments have turned most Arab Spring countries into battlegrounds wherein old geopolitical rivalries deepened and new regional alliances were constructed. Taking Gaza, Syria and Egypt as cases in point, this paper investigates how Ankara and Doha's evolving practical geopolitical reasoning and its domestic and international representations converged to create venues for cooperation and promotion of relations to a level of political alignment.

Introduction

When popular protests in Tunisia began to dismantle a decades-old authoritarian regime, masses in other authoritarian Arab countries grew hopeful that state–society relations in the Middle East would never be the same. Many were optimistic that a radical socio-political transformation was imminent and that the political calculations towards the region would reflect such change.[1] However, for some political analysts the mass protests were no more than a temporary 'Arab spring' wherein genuine demand for justice, better socio-economic conditions and political reform would be subdued by the status quo dynamics.[2] Four years into the Arab Spring protests, the latter view seems to have gained ground with counter-revolutions shaking Egypt, Libya and Bahrain and civil wars wreaking havoc in Syria, Libya and Yemen.

Revolutions and counter-revolutions in the Arab Spring countries have not been shaped by domestic geopolitical dynamics per se. On the contrary, it has been the intervention from regional, and at times global, powers that determined, to a great extent, the trajectory of the protests. In fact, the Arab Spring countries have turned into geopolitical battlegrounds between proxies of several power blocks. Prior to the Arab Spring, there was an evident rivalry between the Sunni and the Shia blocks. The former was dominated by status quo countries hostile to political change and suspicious of the *Shia Crescent*[3] whereas the latter harboured deep mistrust towards the West and its regional allies. As the protest movements intensified, the status quo countries reasoned that tapping into the sectarian discourse would strengthen their position,[4] while the countries of the resistance line relied on the arguments of foreign intervention and Sunni extremism to justify their positions.[5]

In addition to this rivalry, there was a clear regional power vacuum engendered by the Egyptian and Saudi reluctance to assume leadership, which opened up room for new actors to take on a more central role. As the Arab Spring protests bore fruit in Tunisia and Egypt with popular revolutions succeeding, an axis between the two axes, as popularly known in the Arab world, began to arise. Led by Turkey and Qatar, this third block would later include the Muslim Brotherhood (MB) governments in Egypt and Tunisia, as well as Hamas in Gaza. For some analysts, this new political alignment had signalled a rise of the political Islamists. In fact, King Abdullah of Jordan called this newly emergent geopolitical reality the Muslim Brotherhood Crescent,[6] alluding to the Shia Crescent.

Although Ankara and Doha had divergent geopolitical goals and dissimilar material capabilities, they drew closer to each as their practical geopolitical reasoning in the Arab Spring converged greatly. However, this provoked the status quo countries, led mainly by the United Arab Emirates (UAE) and Saudi Arabia, to spoil the emergence of an alliance that would radically challenge their regional status and, arguably, their regimes in the long run. This rivalry engendered a military coup in Egypt, protracted the civil wars in Libya and Syria, and strained relations between the two Sunni groupings, which persisted until more pressing threats, such as the rise of Islamic State (IS) in Syria and Iraq and the Houthi takeover in Yemen, appeared to have created peculiar venues for a cooperation of convenience.[7] In light of these geopolitical rivalries, emerging alliances and shifting enemy–friend depictions, this paper zeroes in on the geopolitical reasoning Turkey and Qatar employed from the onset of the Arab Spring until the present. Analysing the discourse and actions of Turkish and Qatari foreign policy elites towards Gaza, Syria and Egypt, the paper traces both actors' practical geopolitical reasoning and their representations at the domestic and international levels.

The paper is comprised of two parts. The first part provides a theoretical background on practical geopolitical reasoning and how and why political actors construct, present, alter and justify it in times of crises. The second part analyses how the Turkish and Qatari geopolitical reasoning unfolded in three cases: Gaza, where Ankara and Doha began to diverge from the larger Sunni block; Syria, the most important arena where both actors became increasingly involved in the Arab Spring; and finally, Egypt, where both actors' ambitious geopolitical calculations were tested by the regional and international status quo dynamics. This section also investigates how Ankara and Doha's practical geopolitical reasoning evolved at the discourse and action levels vis-à-vis their domestic constituencies and international audiences. The final section concludes the paper with brief observations and policy recommendations.

Geopolitical Reasoning

The concept of practical geopolitical reasoning operates in a similar fashion to that of practical reasoning in psychology.[8] The practitioners of statecraft, statespersons, politicians and military commanders—namely, the agents—employ practical geopolitical reasoning to make sense of crises, construct stories to explain these crises, develop strategies for dealing with such situations and conceptualize potential solutions for them according to the means at their disposal and the values which they hold.[9] The geopolitical reasoning process is operational not only in domestic but also in foreign policy decisions in interrelated ways, with the latter affecting the former and vice versa.

Geopolitical reasoning is a 'political process of representation by which the intellectuals of statecraft designate a world and "fill" it with certain dramas, subjects, histories and dilemmas'.[10] Practical geopolitical reasoning relies on consensual and ordinary assumptions about places and their particular identities, which spatially divides places and people into geographical camps.[11] Utilizing certain narratives replete with binary distinctions, analogies, images and metaphors, geopolitical reasoning renders otherwise complex political realities comprehensible.

Understanding geographical knowledge produced at a multiplicity of different sites and then transforming this into a marketable geopolitical reasoning is a challenge.[12] When faced with domestic or international crises, political actors tend to domesticate this highly complicated geographical reality by reducing it to manageable geopolitical abstractions before they present it to domestic and international audiences. To this end, they need simple, familiar and pragmatic storylines, as well as geographical/ spatial generalizations, wherein they can embed their political objectives and present them easily to the general public. This is crucial for securing public consent and legitimization of political actors' manoeuvres. In explaining the geopolitical reasoning that Iran and Saudi Arabia adopted to deal with the situation in the Arab Spring, Aras and Falk observe:

> The confusing and turbulent regional stage enables policy makers to fashion geopolitical truths for internal consumption and to justify their foreign policy maneuvers. Policy makers simplify the geopolitical reality, produce and reproduce depictions of allies and enemies, and make these practical concerns major drivers and determinants of official policy.[13]

In this regard, discourse analysis is arguably the strongest method for tracing the practical geopolitical reasoning of the political leadership of a country. Political discourse is the arena where decisions are made and legitimized and where actions are taken and justified. Discourse offers valuable hints as to how political actors construct their geographical knowledge, formulate their (geo)political imaginations and visions, as well as 'produce commonsense understandings and pragmatic storylines'.[14] In short, political discourse analysis enables us to understand how political actors mobilize geographical knowledge at the practical level in order to justify potentially contentious political decisions.[15]

Examining the definition and applications of practical geopolitical reasoning leaves one with an important question. Tuathail and Agnew used this concept for understanding how the US government, through its interaction with the opposition and the media in a democratic setting, presented, altered and justified its position on the Bosnian War.[16] More often than not, leadership in classic rentier Arab Gulf monarchies does not need to justify its foreign policy positions before a domestic audience, and therefore, one may deduce that practical geopolitical reasoning may not be an appropriate tool to explain Doha's foreign policy decisions in the Arab Spring. However, this argument ignores another important objective of practical geopolitical reasoning: creating threat–enemy chains for legitimizing certain foreign policy choices before domestic and external audiences.[17] If democratic legitimation and authoritarian manipulation are two extremes of practical geopolitical reasoning, Qatar's geopolitical reasoning can be situated somewhere between the two, arguably closer to the former, as Doha wanted to formulate a foreign policy that is easily communicable and justifiable at both domestic and external levels.

Against this backdrop, the practical geopolitical reasoning in Doha aimed at constructing an official foreign policy that is consistent along a storyline, legitimate and justifiable before the domestic and international audiences. As a small power with deep-rooted security and sovereignty vulnerabilities, yet ambitious regional power projections,[18] Qatar's practical geopolitical reasoning was based on forging trustworthy relationships with a wide spectrum of regional and international players using mediation, conflict resolution and chequebook diplomacy and becoming a leading political actor, whose insecurity would be costly for stakeholders.[19] Doha, with its maverick foreign policy and colossal economic gains throughout the Gulf moment,[20] was quick to take its side along with the revolutionaries. The Qatari leadership saw in the Arab Spring a favourable political condition for enhancing its influence and becoming a central political actor in the region by leading positive socio-political transformation.[21] Doha's hyperactive regional foreign policy, which oftentimes indirectly defied Saudi authority and monopoly over regional political developments, concerned Riyadh.[22]

Similarly, prior to the eruption of the Arab Spring protests, Turkey enjoyed high levels of soft power and socio-economic and political prestige throughout the entire region thanks to its equidistant regional foreign policy and contributions to resolve religio-political tensions, among others, in Iraq and Lebanon. In addition, at the onset of the Arab Spring, Turkey enjoyed favourable perceptions both in the Middle Eastern streets and the Western capitals thanks to its secular democracy and well-functioning liberal economy, which could set a viable model for the region. Against this conducive geopolitical context and eager geographic vision of foreign policy elites, Turkey, a relatively robust middle power with unprecedented regional clout, aspired to transform into a central country, a regional hegemon in Mufti's words,[23] with potential global influence.

Inspired by the zero problems with neighbours policy, Turkish foreign policymakers viewed Turkey as a geopolitically central country with historical, cultural and geographical proximity to the Middle East and its people. Therefore, foreign policymakers in Ankara reasoned that siding with the masses and their democratic demands was the ideal choice to attain Turkey's geopolitical goals. Consequently, Ankara began to promote democracy as an effective panacea for suppressed popular demands. For instance, promotion of democracy was a prevalent message in Erdoğan's election victory speech in 2011:

> Today, the Middle East, the Caucasus and the Balkans have won as much as Turkey ... We will become much more active in regional and global affairs ... We will take on a more effective role. We will call for rights in our region, for justice, for the rule of law, for freedom and democracy.[24]

As the hope the Arab Spring revolutions ignited began to fade with counter-revolutionary forces gaining ground, Turkey's current prime minster and former foreign minister, Ahmet Davutoğlu, announced that Turkey's 'value-based' foreign policy, with particular 'emphasis on democracy and popular legitimacy', would continue.[25] Against this backdrop, Turkey and Qatar viewed the political Islamists, more specifically the MB, as the most likely candidate to ascend to political power. Both actors were well aware that supporting such a grass-roots movement would contribute to the realization of their geopolitical goals.

Utilizing this theoretical framework as a guideline, the following section will trace and examine why and how Ankara and Doha drew increasingly closer to each other and how they presented and justified their position to their domestic and external audiences through the Gazan, Syrian and Egyptian cases.

Gaza: Similar Foreign Policy Approaches

Arguably, Ankara and Doha's similar position on the Palestinian issue prior to the Arab Spring protests was the first signal of a closer relationship. Turkey has repeatedly declared that Hamas is a legitimate representative of the Palestinian people because it won a clear electoral victory in transparent Palestinian elections in 2006. Ankara maintained that inclusion of Hamas in mainstream Palestinian politics would promote the democratization of Hamas while excluding it would bring further radicalization. Turkey and Qatar have repeatedly emphasized responding to popular desire for change and the importance of political reforms and economic development as crucial elements for genuine democracy. Qatari Emir Sheikh Hamad's opening speech at the 2006 Doha Forum is quite telling in this respect:

> The controversy over reform that has started in the Middle East is necessary and must continue until citizens get their due share of political and economic freedom ... Establishing the regional security could not be completed unless democratic practice make progress.[26]

In addition, Ankara argued that ostracizing a democratically elected Hamas would undermine efforts to distance it from the Iranian sphere of influence.[27] At the 2009 World Economic Forum in Davos, current Turkish President and former Prime Minister Recep Tayyip Erdoğan stated:

> If we would like to see democracy take root, then we must respect ... the people who have received the votes ... If it's only Fatah who is present ... that is not going to be sufficient ... Hamas has to be taken into consideration as well because they are a part of that society; they have won an election.[28]

Parallel to Turkey's position, Qatar has extended diplomatic and financial support to Hamas, arguing that branding a democratically elected government as a terrorist organization would bolster the radicals, which would be detrimental to not only the peace process but also the Arab public's belief in democracy.[29] To this end, Sheikh Hamad became the first Arab leader to visit Hamas-controlled Gaza to break the Israeli blockade and declare to the international community that Hamas is a legitimate political entity.[30] Long before the Arab street rose up to demand more democracy and dignity, Sheikh Hamad criticized the international community for punishing Palestinian people for their democratic choices:

> This important Arab experience should be supported and encouraged rather than putting pressure on it or interfering with the right of the people to choose their leaders to threaten to withhold aid to them ... the results of these elections reflects a commitment to what is decided by the collective will and the acceptance of the citizens' free choices.[31]

As the Arab Spring protests were spreading across the Middle East, Qatar was able to broker a reconciliation agreement between Hamas and Fatah in Doha in 2012.[32] The agreement between the two Palestinian factions envisioned creating a unity government, which, according to both Turkish and Qatari practical geopolitical reasoning, would bolster regional security and stability.

The foreign policy elite in Ankara has also demonstrated its support for Hamas at the Justice and Development Party (JDP)'s Fifth Annual Congress in December 2014. Hamas leader Khaled Meshaal was invited to participate in the party's launch of the June 2015 parliamentary election campaign. Domestically, Meshaal's visit was instrumental for the JDP to demonstrate its unwavering support for the oppressed Palestinians in an effort to satisfy its core constituency, which has been known for its sensitivity towards the Palestinian cause. As for the external audiences, Turkish foreign policymakers utilized this invitation to boost Ankara's image as a major regional power with strong democratic credentials, who could convey its message to the region through its own democratic practices. In his speech at the event, Meshaal reiterated Ankara's message strongly by declaring, 'a Turkey of democracy, renaissance, progress, and stability empowers all Muslims'.[33]

What made the Turkish and Qatari positions towards Hamas noteworthy? From a practical geopolitical reasoning perspective, the leadership in both countries were well aware that the Palestinian cause in general and the suffering of Gazans in particular were felt deeply in the Middle Eastern psyche regardless of sectarian or ethnic divisions. By showing support for the Palestinian cause both in words and deeds, Ankara and Doha substantiated their claim for being a voice for Muslims, refusing radicalism, leading positive change, and embracing democracy and moderation. In line with their strong belief that consolidation of security and stability in the Middle East is dependent on responding to popular demands, both actors strove to end the international isolation of Hamas. Although the Turkish and Qatari position on Hamas could be interpreted as an ideological position, it enhanced both actors' international and regional recognition, visibility and soft power capabilities.[34] This was instrumental in winning the hearts and minds of the 'Middle Eastern street' and reinforcing both actors' image as impartial peace brokers. In fact, Turkish and Qatari efforts to incorporate Hamas into the mainstream political processes were eventually acknowledged by US Secretary of State John Kerry when his office requested the help of 'countries that have leverage over the leaders of Hamas',[35] more specifically Turkey and Qatar, to end the Israeli–Hamas conflict in Gaza in June 2014.

Syria: Converging Geopolitical Goals

Turkish–Syrian relations witnessed extraordinary improvement prior to the Arab Spring, whereby Ankara enhanced the legitimacy of its new foreign policy approach. Simultaneously, Doha was establishing an extensive network of diplomatic and economic relations with Damascus with the help of its mediation overtures in Lebanon, where Syria was heavily involved. The relations between Turkey, Syria and Qatar gained new momentum with the 2010 trilateral meeting in Istanbul, where the three leaders, as well as their foreign ministers, voiced identical views concerning some of the most pressing regional issues such as Israeli aggression, the reconciliation between Palestinian factions, political stability in Iraq and Iran's right to possess peaceful nuclear energy.[36] Geopolitically, Syria is the most important door through which Turkey can reach the larger Middle East, as well as the Gulf. The Turkish foreign policy elite was well aware that disruption of this vital opening would deprive the Turkish economy of an immense market. Similarly, Doha had already invested billions of dollars in real estate development and the banking sector in Syria.[37]

Having built cordial personal connections with Damascus, initially both the Turkish and the Qatari leadership advised Bashar Al-Assad to realize rapid democratic reforms in order to weather the Arab Spring protests. However, not only did their advice fall on deaf ears in Damascus but also disturbing images began to appear on various forms of media that could not be ignored. Given Ankara and Doha's reaction to the Arab Spring protests in Tunisia and Egypt, Ankara and Doha could no longer resist the moral and popular pressure mounting against Assad's disproportionate use of violence on peaceful demonstrators. As various factions were being organized into a Syrian opposition in the face of bloody crackdowns, Turkey and Qatar severed their diplomatic relations with Damascus, recognized the opposition as the legitimate representative of the Syrian people and began to develop strategies to topple Assad.[38] Democratic change through political reform as a tool in the Turkish and Qatari practical geopolitical reasoning was replaced with regime change.[39] With this shift, Turkey and Qatar began to pursue a more harmonized proactive foreign policy towards the Syrian crisis.[40]

On the political side, both Ankara and Doha became active advocates of the Syrian opposition. For example, Ankara advocated and facilitated the formation of the Syrian National Council (SNC), while Doha lobbied hard in leading the Arab League to recognize the Syrian opposition. Doha also exerted extensive effort to push for a condemnation of the regime and suspension of its membership at the Arab League in 2011. On the international arena, both capitals emphasized the plight of the Syrian people, urged the international community to recognize the SNC and supported international initiatives, such as the 2012 Kofi Annan and the Arab League peace plans. Militarily, Ankara provided logistics to the Free Syrian Army (FSA), the military wing of the SNC, facilitating their military operations in Syria via Turkish soil.[41]

Increasing the international legitimacy of the opposition occupied an important place in Turkish–Qatari geopolitical reasoning in the Syrian case. Qatari Foreign Minister Khalid al-Attiyah and his Turkish counterpart strove to facilitate the election of a more representative Syrian opposition in November 2012. However, when such an effort was dismissed by the USA and the dissidents in the Syrian opposition on the grounds of its lack of representation, anaemic leadership and being a proxy of Turkey and Qatar, Ankara and Doha decided to recognize the Syrian National Coalition. In response to a question about the newly formed coalition, Davutoğlu remarked 'It's up to Syrians to decide their destiny',[42] which could be taken as a cautious presentation of the Turkish–Qatari attempt to keep the Syrian National Coalition as a representative political body. Moreover, to enhance the opposition's legitimacy and power of representation, Turkey and Qatar pursued a constructive attitude towards the Geneva II Conference in January 2014. During his visit to Doha in December 2013, Erdoğan stated that Turkey and Qatar would ensure that the Syrian opposition attends the peace conference with 'a determined and principled' agenda.[43]

As the Syrian crisis was turning into a civil war, two important tools in the Turkish and Qatari practical geopolitical reasoning grew prominent. First, both Ankara and Doha employed a constant diatribe against the legitimacy of the Assad regime, the enemy who had blood on its hands. In their continuous reproduction of this image, they continued to argue that Assad lost his power to represent his own people and therefore, any anti-regime initiative was justified. At the domestic level, Assad's lack of legitimacy was frequently utilized to keep public support for continuing the anti-regime campaign. In fact, a similar position was later echoed by Kerry supporting the idea of a transitional Syrian government without Assad.[44] Second, both Turkey and Qatar voiced their concern about the plight of the Syrian people, the ally, especially after the chemical attack that was allegedly carried out by the regime forces in Ghouta, a district near Damascus, in August 2013.

As the crisis protracted into a conflict with complicated regional and international meddling and sectarian intricacies, Ankara's geopolitical reasoning began to be coloured by depictions of allies and enemies as well as binary distinctions. On the one hand, Ankara increasingly sounded to side with prevalent sectarian discourse after its criticism of external support for a(n) (Alawite) regime that killed its own (Sunni) people. In October 2014, supporting this perception, President Erdoğan vociferously denounced the Iranian spiritual leader Ayatollah Ali Khamenei:

When we ask why did not you object to the killing of 250,000 people in Syria, he says Assad is the only leader who stands against the Israeli aggression. Have Assad ever shot a single bullet against Israel? 250,000 people are killed and you are still sending weapons and money to them. Can there be such a religious leader?[45]

Erdoğan intensified his diatribe against Tehran when the Houthis seized control in Sana'a. Viewing this as a potential opportunity to express his dismay at increasing Iranian influence and mend fences with Saudi Arabia, Erdoğan questioned Iran's intentions:

Iran is trying to dominate the region. Could this be allowed? This has begun annoying us, Saudi Arabia and the Gulf countries. This is really not tolerable and Iran has to see this ... It has to withdraw any forces, whatever it has in Yemen, as well as Syria and Iraq and respect their territorial integrity.[46]

When the IS brutality began to strengthen Assad and Tehran's arguments, an increasingly critical stance against the Western inaction in Syria began to colour both Ankara and Doha's reading and presentation of the crisis. For example, in an exclusive CNN interview with Amanpour in February 2015, Davutoğlu said 'From the early days of the crisis until now, no other country did more than Turkey; what Turkey did against the attacks, brutal attacks of the regime, as well as against IS.'[47] Davutoğlu was also critical of Western reluctance to act even when the regime used chemical weapons in Ghouta in August 2013: 'He [Assad] used chemical weapons. What happened to him? We [international community] didn't do anything.' In the same interview, Davutoğlu also reminded the public of Turkey's earlier warnings about radicalization of the opposition forces and the role Western inaction played in the rise of IS:

We talked to our European and American colleagues that if there is no solution against these crimes against humanity by the Syrian regime, there will be a rise of radicalism. If others listened to our advice ... today we wouldn't be facing such a big crisis.[48]

Similar depictions were also utilized by the Qatari leadership, who emphasized the lack of Western initiative to resolve the Syrian Crisis. For example, in an interview with CNN in September 2014, Qatari Emir Sheikh Tamim bin Hamad, on allegations about Qatar's role in the rise of IS, criticized the West for failing to understand the root cause of the rise of terrorist organizations in Syria. According to him, the main cause of all this was the regime in Syria. He states, 'We have been saying that from day one, that if we ... stop Bashar committing genocide on his own people, this is where we are going to reach.'[49] In a meeting with President Erdoğan in December 2014, the Emir of Qatar said, 'We criticized Syrian regime's attitude together. We had already warned that the violence of the regime in Syria would lead to the rise of more violent organizations.'[50]

Based on this narrative, several geopolitical dynamics explain why Turkey and Qatar achieved a close cooperation on the Syrian crisis and why such cooperation has not yet born satisfactory results. First, Ankara and Doha genuinely wanted to enhance regional security and stability. By showing a harmonious reaction to the Syrian crisis, both sides aimed to pressure Assad to refrain from upsetting regional security by realizing political reforms and enhancing his popular legitimacy. However, Assad demonstrated an unanticipated degree of authoritarian resilience. Second, close Turkish–Qatari cooperation was augmented by both countries' strong conviction that the MB elements would become the government in post-Assad Syria, and therefore, it was in their best interest to support them. However, the rise of religious extremism and the emerging rivalries within various Syrian factions and their regional patrons such as Saudi Arabia and Qatar[51] weakened Turkish–Qatari potential to influence political change. Third, geopolitically, Turkey and Qatar were disturbed by the increasing regional influence of Iran, and they projected that a new government in Damascus, which would technically bolster Sunni Islamists, would restrain Shia–Iran influence on the Alawite-dominated Syria and Hezbollah-dominated Lebanon.[52] However, they miscalculated the role of religious sentiments in spatializing the crisis, as well as the amount of external diplomatic, economic and military support Damascus would receive.

Egypt: Political Alignment and its Limits

Perhaps the most important political convergence between Ankara and Doha occurred with their support for the rising influence of non-state actors, namely, the moderate Islamists in the region.[53] What started as similar foreign policy outlooks in the early 2000s, swiftly transformed into a practical political alignment. Similar to the Syrian case, Ankara and Doha capitalized on arguments supporting popular will and legitimized their opinions by presenting their support for the revolutionaries in Egypt. In fact, Ankara was the first capital to make an unambiguous call to Hosni Mubarak to yield to legitimate political demands. Emphasizing the demands of the Egyptian people, Erdoğan urged Mubarak to leave power in early February 2011: 'You should listen to the people and their rightful demands ... You should take the necessary steps to satisfy the Egyptian people's demands first ... Demands for freedom cannot be postponed and cannot be neglected.'[54] Ankara and Doha were well aware of Egypt's socio-cultural centrality in the Arab world and its geopolitical significance connecting the Levant, the Gulf and North Africa.

The Egyptian MB government that came to power as a result of democratic elections presented Ankara and Doha with a golden opportunity not only for economic and political cooperation but also for forming an influential partnership essential for achieving their geopolitical goals.[55] Coming from somewhat similar backgrounds and enjoying a vision of more cooperation among Muslim countries, the JDP and its Egyptian counterpart, the Freedom and Justice Party, were keen to maintain close collaboration on various regional issues such as the Palestinian issue.

In addition, the Morsi government and its connections with the MB opposition groups in other Arab Spring countries were invaluable for Ankara on its way to develop better communication lines and project further political influence across the region. In a similar fashion, Doha's geopolitical objective to become an indispensable regional political actor was facilitated by its generous financial support to the Egyptian economy and personal links to the MB foreign policy elite. On the one hand, the Qatari flag and pictures of Sheikh Hamad were flying high in jubilant crowds from Tunisia to Libya to Egypt to Gaza, boosting Qatari self-confidence. On the other hand, Gulf Cooperation Council (GCC) neighbours were mounting pressure on Doha to quit its support for political Islam.

When the Morsi government was ousted by a military junta in the summer of 2013, Ankara's reaction against the military intervention was no surprise. In Ankara's geopolitical reasoning, the new military regime in Cairo was illegitimate: its treatment of the Egyptian people undemocratic and its approach to the Palestinian cause insincere. For example, in a CNN interview in July 2014, Erdoğan stated that 'Sisi is not a democrat ... he is right now a tyrant' and that 'Egypt at this moment does not have a sincere approach to the Palestine issue'.[56] Oversimplifying a complex geopolitical reality that was to become the most profound setback for Ankara's geopolitical goals, Turkey presented its anti-coup arguments on two planes. On the international stage, Turkey maintained that a democratically elected government cannot be forced to concede its power unless it is defeated in fair elections: any other domestic or external intervention is illegitimate and, therefore, unacceptable. In this regard, JDP officials made recurrent references to Western double standards when it comes to democracy in Muslim countries and called on the West to refuse to recognize the military regime. To strengthen their geopolitical narratives, statesmen in Ankara employed binary oppositions of us vs. them, those who stand by democratic principles and human rights vs. those hypocrites who turn a blind eye to the popular will and massacres in Egypt.

In a bitter criticism against the West's silence, Erdoğan, both as prime minister and as president, questioned Western sincerity about democracy in saying, 'If Western countries are not sincere about this issue and if they do not act sincerely, I believe that democracy will be questioned around the world. And we [Turkey] are included in this.'[57] Gulf financers of the military intervention were also targeted by Erdoğan. When King Abdullah declared resolute Saudi support for Al-Sisi in an official statement in August 2014 and accused 'those [namely, Turkey and Qatar] who interfered in Egypt's internal affairs' of 'fanning the fire of sedition' and 'promoting terrorism',[58] Erdoğan ostracized the pro-intervention Gulf monarchies for 'collaborating with the military intervention', 'behaving hypocritically' and 'condoning terrorism'.[59] Similarly, Davutoğlu accused the pro-military coup monarchies of remaining silent in face of oppression in the hands of the region's archaic regimes and conspiring against legitimate governments to deter democracy and to keep the region under the iron fist of autocrats.[60]

Although the initial Qatari reaction to the military takeover in Cairo was similar to the Turkish reaction, it cannot be understood without taking into context the abdication of Sheikh Hamad in favour of his son Sheikh Tamim in June 2013 about a month before the military intervention. As Doha was facing intense pressure from Saudi and Emirati leadership, analysts viewed the Qatari Emir's abdication as a potential signal for a dramatic shift in Qatari foreign policy. However, as Egyptian politics was being reshaped by the military government on the one side and the MB resistance on the other, the new leadership in Doha did not seem to alter its position on the illegitimacy of the military takeover, except in palliative reconciliatory measures such as congratulating the new president, Al-Sisi, and lowering its level of criticism. For about eight months, neither did Doha stop providing sanctuary to major Egyptian MB figures, nor did it completely succumb to the criticism that Al Jazeera serves as a mouthpiece of the political Islamists. Only when the Saudi, Emirati and Bahraini ambassadors returned to Doha in November 2014, ending an eight-month dispute, did Doha appear to restitute its pragmatic foreign policy. Even after the normalization of relations with its GCC neighbours and Egypt, the Qatari leadership continued to emphasize 'supporting the will of the Egyptian people and the country's stability'[61] rather than 'supporting the new regime', arguably in an effort to save face in the domestic and international arenas. Although, the slow shift in Doha's foreign policy positions was regarded as the end of the Turkish–Qatari political alignment by some,[62] others argued that Turkey had to understand Doha's difficult situation and continue to enhance its political, economic and military partnership with Qatar.

The status quo monarchies, who strictly prioritized regime survival above all, were worried that the potential repercussions of the Arab Spring protests could spell the end of their regimes. In their practical geopolitical reasoning, a successful transition to democracy in the larger Middle East could trigger demand for genuine democracy in the Gulf. Therefore, the MB, whom they accused of destabilizing the region through inciting terrorism, had to be outlawed. To counter such a narrative, Turkish and Qatari geopolitical reasoning resorted to using diplomatic, financial and media muscle to boost the Morsi government as the only legitimate representative of the Egyptian people, both throughout the Morsi government and in the post-coup period. For example, Turkey and Qatar loaned billions of dollars to the Morsi government in development assistance, investments or loans while Al Jazeera broadcasted extensive pro-Morsi coverage in order to affect regional and international public opinion. On the domestic level, Turkish politicians, as well as the pro-government media, made analogies to the Turkish experience with past military coups and the following socio-economic difficulties and degradation of basic human rights. Additionally, in an effort to present Turkey's principled stance, Erdoğan frequently and harshly condemned the military regime, and stood by the pro-Morsi demonstrators regardless of its political and economic costs to Turkey.

The Egyptian court's verdict that sentenced the deposed President Morsi and 105 other people to death in May 2015 seems to have unfolded another phase in the Turkish–Qatari alignment. Although the verdict needs to be confirmed by the Grand Mufti, the highest religious authority in Egypt, Erdoğan was one of the first leaders to condemn the decision, branding it as a relapse into the 'old Egypt', which 'lacked democracy'.[63] Making analogies between the hanging of the Turkish Prime Minister Menderes in 1960 by the military junta and the ousted President Morsi in the hands of the Egyptian military, Davutoğlu condemned the verdict and criticized the West for its silence: 'Those who tried to teach us a lesson on freedoms during the Gezi [Park] protests, where are you now?'[64] Similarly, Erdoğan criticized the West for failing to defend democracy:

> What has been done against Morsi and his friends is not acceptable. The world is in self-denial by keeping silent. If you say democracy and election, you should see that this verdict is a sentence given to elections, democracy, and national will.[65]

The Turkish geopolitical reasoning in the Egyptian case appeared to be consistent in prioritizing democracy and popular legitimacy and castigating Western inaction concerning marginalization of Middle Eastern people who aspired for more democracy. In contrast, Qatari geopolitical reasoning demonstrated a slow but considerable shift towards the Saudi position as Doha seemed to have relinquished its unconditional support for the MB in order not to be isolated by its status quo neighbours. This shift was evident in the fact that no statement was made by Qatar to condemn the death sentences—except by Sheikh Qaradawi, who denounced the verdict as 'nonsense' and claimed, 'These rulings have no value and cannot be implemented because they are against the rules of God, against the people's law ... No one will accept it' in an Al Jazeera broadcast.[66] Although Ankara and Doha experienced an unprecedented political alignment around converging geopolitical interests in the Arab Spring, the Egyptian setback seems to have tested the limits of such an alignment beyond expectations.

Conclusion

Turkey and Qatar have emerged as ambitious regional actors with aspiring geopolitical goals against the backdrop of the regional power vacuum and a set of conducive domestic and external political and economic developments. As a regional power, Turkey aspired both to lead imminent socio-political transformation in the region and to project its power across the Middle East. As a small state with security concerns, Qatar pursued a carefully crafted practical foreign policy whereby Doha increased its friendly relations and projected influence over a wide range of political actors. The Arab Spring protests presented an ideal political context whereby both countries could realize their geopolitical goals and wield extensive regional political and economic clout.

Although initial stages of the protests appeared to have earned Ankara and Doha valuable partners, that is, MB governments, subsequent stages witnessed divisions that surfaced along concerns of regime survival and sectarian fault lines. As MB elements enhanced their power in countries undergoing revolutionary protests, Ankara and Doha fell out with other members of the Sunni block, most notably with Saudi Arabia and the UAE, who saw an existential threat in political Islam. In order to maintain domestic and international support for their decisions, the foreign policy elite both in Ankara and Doha employed a dynamic, practical geopolitical reasoning, which spanned from championing democracy to preserving legitimacy to supporting regime change, by active involvement in the crises. To this end, both capitals have used their diplomatic, economic and media clout to present, substantiate, justify and legitimize their foreign policy manoeuvres. Oversimplified geopolitical abstractions, friend–foe depictions and narratives woven around sectarian tensions were utilized to render their positions communicable, acceptable and legitimate. Five years into the Arab Spring process, Turkey and Qatar, despite minor differences, seem to have matured their partnership despite shifting alliances.

The sudden rise of IS terror, potential rapprochement between the West and Iran, and the current instability in Yemen seem to be shifting alliances once more as Riyadh has recently toned down its extreme aversion toward the MB and initiated a plan to form a Sunni front against the Iranian influence. Although the details of this nebulous alliance have yet to unfold, it is perceived that this time the new enemies are actually the old enemies—the Shia and the extremist groups—and the major lines in the emerging narrative will involve oversimplifying geographical reality and reproducing a quite familiar geopolitical discourse replete with sectarian tensions, threat–enemy depictions and shifting alliances.

Disclosure Statement

No potential conflict of interest was reported by the authors.

Notes

[1] A. Bayat, 'The Arab Spring and its surprises', *Development and Change*, 44(3), 2013, pp. 587–601.
[2] D. Held and K. C. Ulrichsen, 'The Arab Spring and the changing balance of global power', *Open Democracy*, 26 February 2014, <https://www.opendemocracy.net/arab-awakening/david-held-kristian-coates-ulrichsen/arab-spring-and-changing-balance-of-global-power> (accessed 15 May 2015).
[3] C. Matthews, 'King Abdullah II of Jordan', *NBC News*, 9 December 2004, <http://www.nbcnews.com/id/6679774/ns/msnbc-hardball_with_chris_matthews/t/king-abdullah-ii-jordan/#.VVb9lfmqqkp> (accessed 12 May 2015).
[4] T. Matthiesen, *Sectarian Gulf: Bahrain, Saudi Arabia, and the Arab Spring that Wasn't*, Stanford University Press, Stanford, 2013.
[5] B. Aras and E. Yorulmazlar, 'Turkey and Iran after the Arab Spring: finding a middle ground', *Middle East Policy*, 21(4), 2014, pp. 112–120.
[6] J. Goldberg, 'The modern king in the Arab Spring', *The Atlantic*, April 2013, <http://www.theatlantic.com/magazine/archive/2013/04/monarch-in-the-middle/309270/> (accessed 11 May 2015).
[7] A. Stein, 'Turkey's Yemen dilemma', *Foreign Affairs*, 7 April 2015.
[8] N. Fairclough and I. Fairclough, *Political Discourse Analysis*, Routledge, New York, 2012.
[9] G. Tuathail and J. Agnew, 'Geopolitics and discourse: practical geopolitical reasoning in American foreign policy', *Political Geography*, 11(2), 1992, pp. 190–204.
[10] Ibid., p. 194.
[11] Gearóid Tuathail, *Critical Geopolitics: The Politics of Writing Global Space*, Routledge, London, 1996.
[12] Tuathail and Agnew, op. cit., p. 195.

[13] B. Aras and R. Falk, 'Authoritarian "geopolitics" of survival in the Arab Spring', *Third World Quarterly*, 36(2), 2015, pp. 322–336.

[14] G. Tuathail, S. Dalby and P. Routledge, *The Geopolitics Reader*, Routledge, Abingdon, 2006.

[15] Tuathail and Agnew, op. cit., p. 191.

[16] Ibid., pp. 190–204.

[17] Aras and Falk, op. cit., p. 322.

[18] A. Echagüe, 'Emboldened yet vulnerable: the changing foreign policies of Qatar and Saudi Arabia', *FRIDE*, July 2014, < http://fride.org/download/WP_123_Emboldened_yet_vulnerable.pdf> (accessed 19 May 2015).

[19] Mehran Kamrava, *Qatar: Small State, Big Politics*, Cornell University Press, Ithaca, NY, 2013.

[20] A. Abdulla, 'Contemporary socio-political issues of the Arab Gulf moment', Kuwait Programme on Development, Governance and Globalization in the Gulf States, Research Paper No. 11, London School of Economics, London, 2010.

[21] K. Ulrichsen, *Qatar and the Arab Spring*, Oxford University Press, Oxford, 2014.

[22] F. G. Gause III, 'Beyond sectarianism: the new Middle East Cold War', Brookings Institution, Washington, DC, 11 July 2014, < http://www.brookings.edu/~/media/research/files/papers/2014/07/22-beyond-sectarianism-cold-war-gause/english-pdf.pdf> (accessed 13 April 2015).

[23] M. Mufti, 'A little America: the emergence of Turkish hegemony', May 2011, < http://www.brandeis.edu/crown/publications/meb/MEB51.pdf> (accessed 13 May 2015).

[24] S. Güste, 'Mandate for a new Turkish era', *New York Times*, 15 June 2011.

[25] A. Davutoğlu, 'Principles of Turkish foreign policy and regional political structuring', Republic of Turkey Ministry of Foreign Affairs, 3 April 2012, < http://sam.gov.tr/wp-content/uploads/2012/04/vision_paper_TFP2.pdf> (accessed 10 May 2015).

[26] S. Hamad, Inauguration speech at the Sixth Doha Forum on Democracy, Development and Free Trade, 11 April 2006, < http://www.qatarconferences.org/new-democracy/newsdetail.php?id=17> (accessed 17 May 2015).

[27] G. Dalay and D. Friedman, 'The AK Party and the evolution of Turkish political Islam's foreign policy', *Insight Turkey*, 15(2), 2013, pp. 123–139.

[28] Erdoğan's speech at Davos Economic Forum, February 2009, < http://www.eutopic.lautre.net/coordination/spip.php?article3976> (accessed 12 May 2015).

[29] B. Haykel, 'Qatar's foreign policy', Norwegian Peacebuilding Resource Centre, Oslo, February 2013, < http://www.peacebuilding.no/var/ezflow_site/storage/original/application/2ec79531a408cf9e5eb93fa5393f8224.pdf> (accessed 16 May 2015).

[30] M. Cevikalp, 'Küçük dev, yeni aktör: Katar' [Small giant, new actor: Qatar], *Aksiyon*, 18 March 2013.

[31] Hamad, op. cit.

[32] P. Akpınar, 'Qatar's regional aspirations: changing mediator role during the Arab Spring', *POMEAS Brief*, No. 6, February 2015.

[33] B. Dabbagh and M. al-Fadilat, 'Hamas leader strengthens alliance with Turkey', *Al-Araby Al-Jadeed*, 29 December 2014.

[34] K. B. Kanat, 'AK Party's foreign policy: is Turkey turning away from the West?', *Insight Turkey*, 12(1), 2010, pp. 205–225.

[35] P. Goodenough, 'State Department defends partnership with Hamas-supporting Qatar', *CNSNews*, 2 December 2014.

[36] 'Assad, Erdoğan and Sheikh Hamad meet in Istanbul', *Syrian News Station*, 9 May 2010, < http://sns.sy/sns/?path=/news/read/13858> (accessed 17 May 2015).

[37] A. Gulbrandsen, 'Bridging the Gulf: Qatari business diplomacy and conflict mediation', MA Thesis, Georgetown University, Washington, DC, 2010, < https://repository.library.georgetown.edu/handle/10822/552827> (accessed 18 May 2015).

[38] P. Beaumont, 'How Qatar is taking on the world', *The Guardian*, 7 July 2012.

[39] Z. Onis, 'Turkey and the Arab revolutions: boundaries of regional power influence in a turbulent Middle East', *Middle East Politics*, 19(2), 2014, pp. 1–17.

[40] T. E. Ozturk, 'Ortadoğu'daki Son Gelişmeler ve Türkiye-Katar İlişkileri: Yeni Bir Sünni Bloğu Mu?' [The latest developments in the Middle East and Turkey–Qatar relations: a new Sunni block?], *TASAM*, December 2011, <http://www.tasam.org/tr-TR/Icerik/4480/ortadogudaki_son_gelismeler_ve_turkiye_-_katar_iliskileri_yeni_bir_sunni_blogu_mu_> (accessed 20 April 2011).

[41] C. J. Chivers and E. Schmitt, 'Arms airlift to Syria rebels expands, with aid from C.I.A.', *New York Times*, 24 March 2013.

[42] S. Erkuş, 'Ankara in talks with Syria's ex-premier', *Hurriyet Daily News*, 6 November 2012.

[43] M. A. Berber, 'Collaboration with Qatar for Geneva 2 conference on Syria', *Daily Sabah*, 5 December 2013.

[44] 'Syria peace talks open with angry exchanges', *PBS NewsHour*, 22 January 2014.

[45] 'Erdoğan'dan Hamaney'e tepki: Böyle bir dini önder olabilir mi?' [Reaction from Erdoğan to Hamaney: can there be such a religious leader?], *Al-Jazeera Turk*, 13 October 2014.

[46] 'Turkish President Erdoğan says can't tolerate Iran bid to dominate Middle East', *Hurriyet Daily News*, 27 March 2015.

[47] M. Krever, 'Turkey willing to put troops in Syria "if others do their part", Prime Minister says', *CNN*, 3 February 2015.

[48] Ibid.

[49] M. Krever, 'Qatar's Emir: we don't fund terrorists', *CNN*, 25 September 2015.

[50] 'Turkey, Qatar share concerns in Syria, Iraq: Erdoğan', *Anatolian Agency*, 19 December 2014.

[51] K. C. Ulrichsen, 'Qatar and the Arab Spring: policy drivers and regional implications', Carnegie Endowment for International Peace, Washington, DC, 24 September 2014, <http://carnegieendowment.org/2014/09/24/qatar-and-arab-spring-policy-drivers-and-regional-implications> (accessed 12 April 2015).

[52] Gause, op. cit., p. 1.

[53] Ö. Pala, 'The evolution of the Turkish–Qatari relations from 2002 to 2013: converging foreign policies, identities and interests', Unpublished MA Thesis, Qatar University, Doha, September 2014.

[54] 'Erdoğan urges Mubarak to heed people's call for change', *Today's Zaman*, 2 February 2011.

[55] B. Gumus, 'Türkiye-Katar İlişkileri', Center for International Strategy and Security Studies, Washington, DC, 3 October 2013, <http://www.usgam.com/tr/index.php?l=807&cid = 2112&konu = 0&bolge = 5> (accessed 16 May 2015).

[56] 'Turkish PM Erdoğan sits down with CNN's Becky Anderson', *CNN*, 24 July 2014.

[57] 'Erdoğan: Batının Mısır tavrı demokrasinin sorgulanmasına yol açar' [Erdoğan: West's attitude towards Egypt will lead to questioning of democracy], *Radikal*, 15 August 2013.

[58] 'Saudi King Abdullah declares support for Egypt against terrorism', *Al Arabiya*, 16 August 2013.

[59] S. Ergin, 'Erdoğan, Suudilerle kopruleri atiyor' [Erdoğan breaking relations with Saudis], *Hurriyet*, 20 August 2013.

[60] R. Falk, 'Turkish PM in conversation, part 1, 2, 3 and 4: the Arab Spring and Turkey's future', *Open Democracy*, 17 December 2014, <https://www.opendemocracy.net/ahmet-davuto%C4%9Flu-richard-falk/turkish-prime-minister-ahmet-davuto%C4%9Flu-in-conversation-part-1> (accessed 11 May 2015).

[61] 'Qatar recalls Cairo envoy over Egyptian suggestion Doha supports terrorism', *Associated Press*, 19 February 2015.

[62] 'Katar–Türkiye İttifakı Bitti, Türkiye Mısır'a Karşı Yalnız Kaldı' [Qatar–Turkey alliance is over; Turkey is left alone against Egypt], *Haberler*, 22 December 2014, <http://www.haberler.com/katar-turkiye-ittifaki-bitti-turkiye-misir-a-6796624-haberi/> (accessed 16 May 2015).

[63] A. Sahin, 'Turkey lambasts Morsi's death sentence, calls for global reaction', *Daily Sabah*, 17 May 2015.

[64] 'Davutoğlu attacks Turkish media over coverage of Morsi death sentence', *Today's Zaman*, 17 May 2015.

[65] 'EU denounces Morsi verdict, Ankara to take case to UN', *Hurriyet Daily News*, 18 May 2015.

[66] B. Tufft, 'Senior Muslim cleric Qaradawi denounces death sentences against Mohamed Morsi and Muslim Brotherhood leaders as nonsense', *The Independent*, 17 May 2015.

Özgür Pala is a PhD student in the Gulf Studies Program at Qatar University. His research interests include (state) identity, security and foreign policymaking in the Gulf. He earned his Master's degree in Gulf Studies from Qatar University in 2014. His MA thesis is titled 'The Evolution of the Turkish–Qatari Relations from 2002 to 2013: Converging Policies, Identities and Interests'. Previously, he earned a Master's degree in English Language Teaching from University of Oregon, USA, in 2005.

Bülent Aras is Senior Scholar and Coordinator of the Conflict Resolution and Mediation stream at Istanbul Policy Center, Professor of International Relations in the Faculty of Arts and Social Sciences at Sabancı University and Global Fellow at Wilson Center. He is the Academic Coordinator of POMEAS (Project on the Middle East and Arab Spring). His current research interests include the geopolitics of the Arab Spring, non-state actors in peacebuilding, and bridging the gap between theory and practice in foreign policy. His recent work has been published in *Third World Quarterly*, *Middle East Policy*, *International Peacekeeping*, *Political Science Quarterly*, *International Journal*, *Journal of Balkan and Near Eastern Studies* and *Journal of Third World Studies*.

The Impact of the Arab Spring on the Gulf Cooperation Council

Larbi Sadiki

It is apposite to interrogate the notion of 'monarchical exceptionalism' when testing the idea that the 'Arab Spring' has not affected the so-called 'ruling bargain' in the Gulf Cooperation Council (GCC). The Arab Spring élan is presented in this paper as the sole dynamic with attributes of 'exceptionalism'. It constitutes a moment of history that continues to rock the decaying pan-Arab body politic to its foundations, be it in varying degrees. It may be argued that there is an undeniable 'Arab Spring effect', which has unleashed a largely uncontrollable chain of events, stimulating or setting in motion the idea of change, civic and/or unruly. From this perspective, the Arab Spring can best be labelled as 'midwife' to all kinds of aspiring actors, forces, voices and discourses whose quest for change had been put on the back burner when the uprisings erupted in 2011. States are no exception. To elaborate on this line of argument, a twofold analytical agenda is followed. Firstly, change is contextualized, before and after the Arab Spring, addressing how politics is organized in the Arab region. Secondly, the GCC's 'story' with the Arab Spring is disaggregated, with special reference to Qatar's bold new politics.

Introduction: The Age of the Arab Spring

This section gives a brief but critical account of the phenomenon of the 'Arab Spring'. This it does via an unorthodox interpretation of why the Arab Spring élan represents a departure point from many 20th-century revolutions. Most scholarly accounts find a correlation between the Arab Spring and transformation or change. This is one assumption informing this paper. There are hints of transformation in the momentum built, for instance, for democratization as part and parcel of the Arab Spring. However, this is not the case with the Gulf Cooperation Council (GCC). At the level of society, there is the dynamic of unruliness, defiance against and resistance to authoritarian rule, the common denominator in all Arab uprisings, whether successful (producing ousters in Egypt, Libya, Tunisia and Yemen in 2011) or incomplete and/or bloody (Bahrain and Syria). Kuwait provides another interesting case study, given the electoral and parliamentary continuity present in this GCC member state. Kuwait has been rocked by a different form of protests (in support of the right of equal citizenship of stateless groups, namely, the Bedouin, and greater accountability and transparency especially by the ruling Al-Sabahs) from those experienced by Bahrain (the main cry of the country's Shi'a, including the Al-Wifaq organization, is power-sharing). Therefore, the change in the context of the Arab Spring should not be reduced to a notion of democratic politics: that is, an understanding cemented to conventional templates and practices; invariably assumed to culminate in law-based contestation, participation and supportive civic publics; and non-personalist systems that are either contracted to run government or organize orderly opposition periodically and peacefully. The gist of the account attempted here is to draw attention to an important aspect of political activity within the Arab Spring: the unruliness informing anti-authoritarian protest and resistance by society and the attempts to respond to them at the state level. The crux of this unruliness is public mobilization and organization through self-configuration through one's own language, ideals, strategies and coalitions. Rebellion against instruments of authoritarianism does not necessarily have a democratizing effect in an institutional sense. Unruliness, civic and violent, is hypothesized as a challenge to existing mediums of systemic reproduction by the postcolonial power-holders. In the quest for dignity (*karamah*) and freedom (*hurriyyah*), unruliness is society's agential deployment against the 'occupiers' of the authoritarian state. This has not featured in the politics of GCC citizens or nations, bar Kuwait and Bahrain. This is one reason why the discussion will be mostly angled at understanding the response crafted by the Qatari elite to manage whatever pressure or opportunity for change the Arab Spring has brought forth. More generally, reference to the Arab Spring, interchangeably used with the uprisings of 2011 and subsequent chain reactions in the region, is associated here with the dynamic of political change, real or latent. One ubiquitous feature is widespread 'unruliness'. Apart from informally engendering bottom-up notions of sovereign identities and participatory citizenship in the public squares of protest, this unruliness, especially via civic and peaceful forms, has facilitated the people's coming together to challenge authoritarian regimes and their attendant structures of power. This produced outright ousters such as that of Hosni Mubarak in Egypt in February 2011.[1] Thus, the regimes' routinized notions of stability, loyalty and deference, for instance, are traded for spontaneously conceived practices, thought and language, mostly revolving around notions of social justice, freedom and dignity. The Arab Spring has ushered in an age of mobilization for change by societies (Bahrain, Kuwait, Yemen, etc.) as well as by states (e.g. Morocco, Qatar, Tunisia).[2] Stability cedes to fluidity, loyalty gives way to hostility and rebellion, and deference to resistance. To borrow a term from Paulo Freire's *Pedagogy of the Oppressed*, 'critical consciousness' is thus forged and invented in the public squares of protest as a necessity to counter the hegemonic order with action, thought, and all kinds of signifiers of opposition and resistance. While instantaneous and spontaneous, the critical consciousness summoned in the public squares of protest seems to generate (e.g. Egypt and Tunisia in 2011) the necessary democratic agency to unify the rebellious publics around a spirit beckoning new beginning. Taking a stand as a united public with unified practice, thought (perhaps dreams) and terminology constitutes an initial step towards reconstitution of subjectivities and rejection of subjection to authoritarian rule and rulers. However, as in the example of Qatar, states have also galvanized their resources, institution and leadership for the cause of guided and managed transformation.

Contextualizing the Dynamic of Change

It is impossible to deny 'change', incremental or radical, in the context of the 'Arab Spring'. No other event has rocked the Middle East to its foundation as much as has these uprisings. Its impact is equal to the discovery of oil in Iran (1908) and Saudi Arabia (1938), the founding of Israel in 1948, Egypt–Israel Camp David Accords (1979), the Declaration of Principles (1993), 9/11 (2001) and the sacking of Baghdad (2003). Many Arab observers are therefore validated in thinking that only independence from the yoke of colonialism shares historical parity with the Arab uprisings of 2011. Both represent emancipatory moments separated by decades of postcolonial misrule by indigenous elites, of which the likes of Ben Ali, Mohamed Hosni Mubarak and Mu'ammar Gaddafi were quintessential examples of dictators swept from power by the 2011 protest movements—unprecedented politically in the Arab Middle East (AME). Hence, a good departure point is to contextualize, as well as reflect on, the still unfolding fervour spawned by the 'Arab Spring'—not as yet possessing the hindsight of historical *longue durée*.

The postcolonial 'story' of political *power* unfolds through a hegemon, that is, the 'over-stated Arab state'.[3] Ayubi uses this term to record how the Arab state has historically invested itself with all the attributes of power (coercive, financial, legal, tribal, ideological, informational, social, etc.). It has left society with little shared space for normalizing state–society relations, and even less space for societal contests of state power. Since its emergence into territorial existence, the Arab postcolonial state's design of this brand of statecraft fulfils what might be called 'total politics'—the practice of 'totalizing' political activity hindering the rise of potential rival centres of power. That is, a field or margin of civic and oppositional existence with a notable blind spot: societal autonomy. This is the space where society strikes back to invent the vocabulary of self-recognition and self-existence, as well as the attendant thought-practice congenial to speaking back and engaging political power. Therein lies the promise of negotiating the substance of change, its terms and its strategies. In their struggles to effect change, Arab societies have historically capitalized on the space vacated by state power. In every retreat/ absence by the state, there emerges the potential for advancement/presence by society, as if (state) 'zero-power' equates with (societal) 'positive power', at least potentially.

One key idea advanced here is that the postcolonial political organization that preceded the Arab Spring became too ossified: elitist, exclusionary, reliant on distribution or coercion as means of reproducing power. In this regard, the only distinction to be noted is that republican systems' reliance on coercion far outweighs that of monarchies, especially GCC member states. Integral to political organization was the absence of serious safety valves that allow society channels of venting anger. 'Explosion' was a matter of time. For example, in December 2010, a Tunisia fruit vendor, Mohamed Bouazizi, became the trigger.[4] Thus, any narration of the context of the Arab Spring would be incomplete without accounting for the state of political organization in the pre-Arab Spring political setting, as argued below.

Students of politics in the Arab setting are presented with key challenges when addressing the state of political organization. There are two intertwined reasons for this. Firstly, political organization must be accounted for in a context quite distinctive from that found in consolidated democracies as well as newer democracies of the type that have evolved from second and third waves of democratization as explicated by Huntington.[5] In these settings, political democratization has benefited from longer stints of nation- and state-building, as well as struggles that enabled civic bodies to carve out a margin of existence, generally functioning as a bulwark against the state by partaking in competitive politics. Secondly, by and large, from an anthropological perspective, the actual communal or societal framework within which the structure of politics takes shape is itself subject to different types of loyalty, agents, regulation, allocation of resources and value assignment. In the AME, the organization of politics is complicated not only by authoritarianism[6] but also by deep-rooted primordial practices (such as in the GCC where ruling houses lead political organization). This has made status, influence, input, leadership and distribution in the realm of power among 'citizens' within any given Arab-organized political community almost irreversibly unequal. Michael Herb uses the term 'all in the family'.[7] In fact, the meaning of politics, as put succinctly by Lasswell nearly 80 years ago, 'who gets what, when, how' may be handicapped by the absence of fair rules of engagement and rule of law that engender equal citizenship.[8] Michels contends that even under consolidated democratic regimes where political organization is established and professionalized, oligarchical tendencies do not completely disappear.[9] There is no politics without organization. When organized, politics facilitates the business of government, framing it in ways that democratizes leader–citizen and state–society relations. Thus, it renders the whole political vocation of 'who gets what, when, how' more subject to norms of equality, transparency, accountability and legality. Political organization is in some readings assumed to have the potential to 'be a source, in many cases and in many ways, of democratization'.[10] All institutions that advance democracy by way of facilitating processes conducive to the practice of politics pertain to the realm of political organization, which exists in both democratic and non-democratic systems. Specifically, political organization refers to all institutions and units that belong either to political society or civil society, governmental and non-governmental, competitive and non-competitive, local and national, formal and informal, top-down and bottom-up, as part of pressure or interest networks, advocacy work or political parties, and which by virtue of function are integral to the overall political process in a given state. The chief observation to make here is that political organization contributes to the overall performance of a political system, and is itself informed by the nature of a given polity's terms of engagement—be they based on political deference or participative politics. Participative politics is not a common feature of Arab political systems, both before and after the emergence of the Arab Spring. Participative politics denotes the presence of a degree of democracy. Huntington's conventional and minimalist definition classifies a given political system as democratic when 'its most powerful collective decision-makers are selected through fair, honest and periodic elections in which candidates freely compete for votes and in which virtually all the adult population is eligible to vote'.[11] Implied within this definition is the set of civil and political liberties needed to facilitate not only the practice of politics in general but also the electoral process. Political change or transformation is hardly driven bottom-up, by the people, including in the GCC. However, what must be recorded here is that when accounting for 'change' in the context of the Arab Spring, the pressure created, directly or indirectly, has motivated even risk-averse systems, such as Qatar, to consider political fine-tuning as a way of revamping the ruling bargain.

In all Arab formulations of the ruling bargain, power ended up being reconfigured through 'national mentors', who in essence were tribal leaders (e.g. Ibn Saud), army generals (e.g. Nasser, Gaddafi, Ali Abdallah Salih) or demagogues (e.g. Bourguiba). Thus politics did not require the development of shared values, democratic norms, rules governing competition and participation in politics—nor did the very notion of power-sharing emerge as part and parcel of the 'cake of civic culture' underpinning political organization.[12] The common denominator, to varying degrees, is that of leadership acting as a national mentor. What might not be generalizable, as far as these assumptions go, is the degree and source of legitimacy that determine the nature of political leadership. Here claims can be made for and against the degree of and type of 'charisma' a given leader possessed. In this context, Ibn Saud relied on a brand of traditional charisma in which tribal genealogy coupled with preference for an Islamized polity and performance legitimacy (founder of the state) helped his rise to power. The inheritors of his throne varied in terms of charisma and reputation as credible leaders (e.g. King Faisal due to pan-Arabism and pan-Islam). Nasser's political feats in nationalizing the Suez and mounting a sustained political rhetoric noted for its anti-colonial (including guardianship over the Palestinian cause) and pan-Arab substance helped solidify his stranglehold over the reins of power.

The fierce contests against the hegemonic 'imagined communities' of the AME within the realm of the void allow for 'imagined communities' in reverse. That is, they signal the onset of the de-imagining of the existing hegemonic 'imagined communities', seeking their overthrow for being parochial, private–public, privatized and primordialized whilst still claiming a universal nationhood of sorts and inhibiting free choice in the exercise of 'power over'. To re-state Benedict Anderson,[13] nations or communities are imagined through a number of processes:

(1) De-primordialization, that is, the 'imagining' or 'inventing' of a community supersedes kinship ties and close knowledge and association of a clan or tribe. Hence, 'all communities larger than primordial villages of face-to-face contact ... are imagined'.[14] Anderson notes how the 'image of communion' is maintained in territorially vast and populous nations, and this happens not through close contact or informal ties but rather it happens and 'lives' in 'the minds' of a given nation's members.[15] The syllabus, the media and the myths erected to celebrate nationalism all contribute to the imagining and confirming of 'imagined communities'.

(2) Nationalization of identity and belonging: imagined nations pander to nationalist 'ethnocentricity'. As Anderson puts it, the image of communion is inevitably exclusionary of 'imagined' otherness—of other nations or for that matter of humanity as a whole.

> The most messianic nationalists do not dream of a day when all the members of the human race will join their nation in the way that it was possible, in certain epochs, for, say, Christians to dream of a wholly Christian planet.[16]

(3) De-divinization of the newly 'imagined' nations and states (owing to the ascendance of Enlightenment and revolutionary rationality, as Anderson points out): it is within the precincts of nations and territorial self-identification and imagining that religions seek their own brand of 'communion' with God, as if the 'imagined' state is a new quasi-transcendental in its own right, not in need of a rival deity.[17]

(4) Indeed, having de-divinized religion, the new Enlightenment-based rationality mythologized and sacralized the 'imagined' nationalist community (a 'fraternity' or association of compatriots) as a 'deep, horizontal comradeship' to die for in the name of patriotism. Once recruited to the 'imagined' community, passions take over. Self-sacrifice becomes a further baptism of patriotism, adding to the 'image of communion'. Anderson is baffled by the firm grip imagining a myth and dying for it holds as part of the imaginings of the edifice that is 'imagined' nationalism. For its sake, it has been 'possible, over two centuries, for so many millions of people, not so much to kill, as willingly to die for such limited imaginings'.[18]

The imagining of the postcolonial community or nationhood has more or less followed a similar trajectory in most Arab states. The itinerary of the power bidders and new 'occupiers' of the postcolonial state have from day one set out to dismantle primordial association and symbols of identification and anchors (and even arms in many instances) in the name of centralization and modernization. The passing of a type of traditional correctness after the postcolonial era has also relegated religion to a secondary role. Literally, to use Eric Hobsbawm's phrases, the age of postcolonialism has been at once an 'age of revolutions' (by free officers, pan-Arabists, secularists and eventually Islamists) and of 'extremes'[19] (national vs. tribal, modern vs. traditional, universal vs. parochial, etc.). The new rallying myths through which the newly born 'imagined communities' are to be mediated exalt the state and loyalty to its centre. Patriotism has demanded loyalty, sacrifice and modern rationality, as opposed to the rationality of religion and tradition. Just as socialism and social justice during this time furnish additional rallying myths, imperialism and backwardness lace the imagined communities' official transcripts with antitheses, necessary 'enemies' to rally newly nationalized identities around the centre.

Anderson's four processes that have collectively constructed and entrenched the 'imagined community' are more or less coming unstuck. Rather, and more precisely, they were witnessing reversal, in varying degrees, throughout the Arab region prior to the eruption of the Arab Spring. Such a reversal signalled retreat in the original pristine aura and awe of nationalism. The multitude that once substituted nation for tribe, clan, family or other primordial association, is today having second thoughts. Many do already join the swelling march back from the 'imagined community' and towards the protection, certainty and anchorage of these primordial associations. The GCC is spared this transformative trajectory. The brand of nationalism embraced and cultivated does not smack of inhospitality to primordial association and forms of loyalty; nor does it shun religion in maintaining a kind of 'moral glue' and a legitimating force enabling smooth reproduction of state power, with only limited challenges by society (e.g. al-Qaida in the Kingdom of Saudi Arabia—KSA).

As an example, to an extent the fusion of religion and politics in the founding of the Saudi state has served to defuse two potentially contested areas that have to do with political change: the legality of the state and the legitimacy of the power-holders. When the Qur'an is the 'constitution'; when the *Shari'ah* is the law of the land; when Western-modelled institutions (political parties, trade unions) are noted for their absence; and when the learned scholars of the Wahhabi creed continue to under-write political power, the message is that the state's *raison d'être* and 'Godly' values are self-evident. What is most specific about the Saudi fusion of religion and politics is the control of religion by the state, not vice versa. Because the monarch amasses absolute powers (political, economic and coercive) in his hands, his prerogative is without bounds. In theory, the *Shari'ah* reigns supreme. In practice, however, it is the King's prerogative not only to control the clerical 'caste' by fiscal means (they are state employees) but also to appoint them in the first place. It is, accordingly, inconceivable that the King entrusts religious affairs to hostile learned scholars or *ulama*. Conversely, scholars tied to power structures through patronage–clientelism do rarely place their status and the privileges attached to it in jeopardy in the pursuit of their own political agendas or that of an 'opposition'. This dynamic has been most instrumental in stemming the tide of challenges to the ruling house. Note, for instance, how the fusion of religion and politics lends itself to co-option of the religious order by the royal house. The royal house's appointment in the early 1990s of the Imam (chief religious authority and prayer leader) of al-Haram Mosque (Mecca), Shaykh Salih Bin Abdullah Al-Humayd, to the Consultative Council's presidency is evidence of the manipulation and control of religion and religious authorities by the state. More than ever before, since 9/11 the royal house has relied on the religious establishment to under-write political power as well as keep in check religious 'opposition'.

Prior to the Arab Spring, the arrival of Western troops to the Gulf region (1991) and their involvement in two wars (1991 and 2003) are key benchmarks in the Saudi political calendar. One of the resulting political 'triggers' is the rise of 'opposition' and 'challenge' against the state. Both terms are used here very loosely and interchangeably. Generally, 'opposition' is not part and parcel of the Saudi 'cake of custom'. If political culture is a set of tendencies shaped by tradition, norms, symbols or historical memories, then nothing in it suggests propensity towards political opposition in KSA. However, contests abound. They abound even within the royal house itself. The tendency in the KSA is to refer disputations to tribal adjudication, deliberation of the elders, inter-tribal marriages and consensus-building. Consensus-building, as well as containment of 'unruly' opposition, has been assigned more recently to the National Dialogue Forum sponsored since 2003 by the then Crown Prince Abdullah, the late King Abdullah (ruled 2005–15). Note how KSA is the only country where a traditional and indigenous mechanism has been invented to rehabilitate al-Qaida operatives into society through an amnesty negotiated with tribes, judges, scholars and officialdom. In terms of thought the tendency is to adopt the Islamic legal position devised by medieval jurisprudence that *fitnah* (conflict) is the chief enemy of Islam. Keeping the *Ummah* (Islamic Community) united, for the greater sake of religious continuity, far outweighs potentially divisive and conflictual dissidence even if it is at the expense of principles such as just rule. According to this reasoning obedience to unjust rule is preferable to rebellion that leads to conflict.

Opposition in the form of organized and licensed political activity for the advocacy of alternative policies or political representation on behalf of partisan interests does not exist in KSA. All expression and representation of conflicting ideas is proscribed and more often than not punished. Consequently, 'challenge' is a milder term that describes fairly accepted practices of advocating change loyally and from within the system, thus tending to persuade the powers that be to adopt reforms as if they emanated from the state. To an extent, this route followed by King Abdullah has empowered the National Dialogue Forum to be a type of 'chamber' or 'court' for airing dissident opinion within strictly framed conditions controlled by the state. The aim is reform under the condition of national unity, sanctity of Islam (Wahhabi), and allegiance to the royal house and the rejection of violent trends of thought and praxis. This is a move that is motivated both by motives of self-preservation as well as gradual reform that may lead to partial political inclusiveness. The municipal elections of 2005 may be regarded as the first tangible achievement of the dialogue mechanism invented by the late King Abdullah. The elections were held over three phases: 1–10 February for Riyadh and surroundings, 3 March for five regions and the last phase was on 21 April for the remaining seven regions in KSA. In total, 178 councils were involved and 592 seats were contested. Even if business and religious elites worked together and won these elections in the final analysis, the elections constituted a first taste of 'democracy' in KSA and 'tests' of political competition and participation. By any standards, they were an important benchmark in Saudi state-building that preceded the Arab Spring.

The state had to react. The pressure from the international community with the agenda of democracy promotion and from home for reform and stemming the tide of *takfeer* (relegation of fellow Muslim to the realm of unbelief) and *irhab* (terrorism) combined to galvanize the rulers into steering the state into dialogical and inclusive conflict management and containment modes of operation. Indeed, *takfeer* and *irhab* are the most dangerous trends of thought and praxis in KSA. They are interrelated. To engage in the act of *takfeer* and 'excommunicating' co-religionists by non-establishment clerical hardliners is to invite or inspire their followers, many of whom are none other than the graduates of the Islamic institutions and universities, to kill those declared to be non-believers.

However, even KSA has not been immune from the events of the Arab Spring. Regardless of how the message of emancipation integral to the Arab Spring 'travels', manifests itself or mutates socially and politically, it seems to resonate with wide publics within and without the region. The Arab Spring has inspired the masses at the same time that it has struck fear among autocrats across the region. Protests are spearheaded by both individuals and groups in these countries. The periodic protests of increasing frequency by Saudi women drivers is symptomatic as are the individual voices of bloggers and poets. And that spooks the state's security apparatuses. Thus, the reality lurking behind the veil of appearance is not pleasant.[20] Perhaps, abundance of natural resources combined with supernormal surplus extracted from a seemingly infinite supply of cheap labour from South East Asia has enabled the oil monarchies to set up a system of economic privilege and buy the acquiescence of their nationals. The unusual amount of wealth enjoyed by the oil-exporting Gulf States has propelled the ruling elite into adopting a twofold strategy to 'deal with' the prospect of contagion. On the one hand, it has led to the adoption of irrational or draconian measures. The Qatari government, clearly far more liberal than fellow GCC member states, gave a life sentence to Mohammad ibn al-Dheeb al-Ajami, a poet who wrote a poem in 2012 entitled 'Tunisian Jasmine', supporting the uprisings in the Arab world.[21] The sentencing of the Saudi blogger, Raif Badawi, to 1000 lashes and 10 years in prison is another glaring example of the brutal silencing of protest. The joint Saudi and United Arab Emirates (UAE) intervention (14 March 2011) in Bahrain and the 3 July 2013 Saudi–UAE backed military coup in Egypt combined with massive aid packages are complementary measures designed to contain people-driven system reforms. Only a limited dialogic process between the Sunni ruling elite and the Shi'a majority was facilitated by neighbouring states, that is, a process that redistributes power and welfare in a way that produces a win–win outcome (positive-sum game) for the power-holders and civil society. On the other hand, there is a continuous tendency by some GCC states to deploy their ability to bribe entire national populations into silence. In the wake of the Arab Spring, the Gulf States, like Saudi Arabia, enhanced subsidies and other welfare payments for nationals.[22] The measures to appease the national population are not only financial. Qatar has introduced a measure of inclusiveness. For instance, women were granted the right to vote and run in the 2015 municipal elections without the permission of their male guardians. The Arab Spring's absence, thus far, in countries such as Saudi Arabia suggests an eerie presence!

No 'Monarchical Exceptionalism': Qatar?

Orientalism as an attitude or a mode of speaking and writing about the Middle East still persists.[23] Orientalist narratives have historically relegated the AME to a sphere of irrelevance, ahistoricity and exile from the realm of civility and modernity—however understood. Theses of authoritarian 'resilience' have dogged the Middle East for the greater part of postcolonial history.[24] The Arab Spring poses a huge problem for conventional wisdom on the Middle East (or 'Orient') as a discursive formation produced by some Orientalists. Specifically, it warrants serious interrogation of all 'exceptionalism', even when political management is manifested as monarchical authoritarianism.[25] The notion of 'monarchical exceptionalism'[26] may be limited in its explanatory power in that it does not go far enough to account for the full gamut of grades of change that percolate into the system, subtly and otherwise. In one definition, monarchical exceptionalism partakes of three dimensions:

> one that links the historical legacy of domestic choices with a permissive international environment. First, many of these royal houses have historically mobilized cross-cutting coalitions of popular support, coalitions that have helped to forestall mass opposition and to bolster the ruling family against whatever opposition has emerged. Second, most have also reaped ample rents from oil or foreign aid, allowing them to pay for welfare and development programs meant to alleviate public discord. Finally, when all else fails, these kingdoms have enjoyed the backing of foreign patrons.[27]

The state of Qatar bucks the above formulation. This poses a problem for using the notion of monarchical exceptionalism in terms of survival and aversion to change to impose a blanket explanation. Saudi Arabia and UAE, for instance, have been labelled counter-revolutionary in their approach to the Arab Spring. Oman is aloof and cautious, and, as always, more or less neutral. Bahrain, for obvious reasons, does not welcome the defiance encouraged by the Arab Spring. Like Bahrain, Kuwait has had its own protests that cannot be isolated from Arab Spring happenings in terms of galvanizing the street into action and protests. Yom and Gause III's usage of three categories under a blanket definition leaves much to be desired. The obvious anomaly, of course, is Qatar, simultaneously being the host of the largest US base in the Gulf region and also the Arab Spring's most vocal champion. The tiny emirate showered billions of dollars into Egypt prior to Abdulfattah el-Sisi's 3 July coup. Its backing of Libya went beyond soft power, eventually committing medical support and training units to the anti-Gaddafi forces in the lead-up to the fall of the regime in 2011. This has partly given Qatar the distinction of a transitional model, sharing the features noted by Yom and Gause III, particularly its presence in scales that out-class larger Gulf and Arab states on a scale that is far beyond disproportionate to its diminutive geographical size.

The rise of Qatar is literally epic and meteoric, seeming in the foreseeable future to be irreversible. From the late 1990s, the bliss of anonymity ceded to publicity. When launched in 1996, Al Jazeera shattered the silence of the Arab 'public sphere'; and a new brand of pragmatic, proactive, buoyant and bold rule in the tiny gas-rich state became noticeable. Qatar was on the verge of making a big entry into the global hall of political, informational, diplomatic and business 'celebrity'. With increased visibility comes close scrutiny, curiosity and inevitably the kind of conspiratorial thinking that accompanies world-stage political status—especially when the species of state is Arab, Muslim, traditional and inhabits the politically tempestuous waters of the Gulf and borders the 'conflict-prone' Middle East region. The Arab Spring accentuated this status. If Saudi Arabia wears the label of a counter-revolutionary actor, Qatar is precisely its antithesis (and prior to the advent of King Salman almost the nemesis) in terms of Al Jazeera satellite TV coverage of the Arab Spring and unfettered aid to the cause of revolutions in countries such as Egypt, Libya and Tunisia. However, when it comes to Bahrain, Qatar toes the Saudi line, abstaining from any rhetoric or actions that can be interpreted to side with the protests in a country that is a Saudi protégé.

In demystifying Qatar, the paper seeks to shed light on the identity of the tiny Arab Gulf State and the key elements integral to explication of the status, motifs and the undeniable 'prowess' of a once powerless Arab state. To this end, the paper argues, against the gist of much conspiratorial thinking out there, that Qatar may somehow be 'scheming' to 'take over' the economies or control the leaders of Arab states, especially in the aftermath of its active championing of Arab revolts in Egypt, Libya and Tunisia. Qatar is a doggedly autonomous state. Having the advantage of financial bounty, clarity of purpose and direction, and enhanced security, it typifies an attitude of 'who dares wins' in the global arena. A minimalist framework comprised of a set of four angles is used here to elaborate upon these preliminary observations: explanatory, programmatic, orientative and evaluative.

Qatar: The Explanatory Dimension

It is simple. In order to contextualize Qatar's rise is owed, largely but not solely, to explanatory insight. This is where the rulers have hit the bull's eye. Qatar is both simple and complicated. Simple in the sense that it lacks two vital elements of power projection: critical mass (the indigenous population is less than 300,000 in the 2014 census) and landmass (which presents limitations, including scant water reserves). However, Qatar sits on the third largest gas reserves in the world (after Russia and Iran). No other country shares Qatar's comfort in the knowledge that income for the next 100 years is guaranteed. This is an act of geographical coincidence. However, there is nothing left to coincidence as far as political calculus is concerned: Qatar partly derives its increased influence from its ability to convert oil wealth into tangibly augmented power ratios in the international arena. Thus, through explanatory insight, the leadership through knowledge of such ingredients could plan development, road map political action, and design the values and criteria needed for success. To this end, financial resources are put to optimum use through a reciprocal synergy: money in the service of ideas and ideas serving well-spent money. Qatar derives added value from this equation, politically, economically, culturally and in terms of its security needs. Through this explanatory insight, Qatar has been able to balance the traditional and the modern, the domestic and the regional, the local and the global, and the national and the international. The upshot of this explanatory insight, Qatar has, further, treaded a gradual metamorphosis from the tribal to the national, from the national to the international and from the international to the transnational. It is today a quintessential example of a rising brand of symmetrical nationalism engineered without the trauma of violent colonialism or ill-thought 'isms' that afflicted more established states in the Arab region. Kamrava refers to Qatar's use of 'subtle' power as a form of smart capacity embodying agency to surge ahead and upgrade its status.[28] It is the country that was the most receptive to the Arab Spring because partly it has helped craft and cultivate it, in the first place, by lending airtime to dissidents, secularist and Islamists, and was the country that welcomed the uprisings in 2011 with open arms. In this regard, Qatar was ahead of the learning curve when the Arab Spring erupted.

Qatar: The Programmatic Angle

Qatar, relative to its Gulf neighbourhood, is a country that works. Countries do not function within a vacuum. There is a visionary edge. It is this edge that places Qatar today in the centre of the vortex of events that are unfurling in the wider region—namely, the 'Arab Spring'. In addition, and more importantly, this edge has given Qatar a distinct voice in regional and global affairs (rooting on behalf of Arab and Muslim causes) as well as a pole position as far as regional and international good governance indices are concerned. Given the pan-Arab diplomatic sclerosis, partly due to the passive role of Egyptian foreign policymaking under the ousted regime of Mubarak and incoherence with Saudi foreign policy, debilitated by an ailing leadership and ill health of the Foreign Minister, Saud al-Faisal, Qatar boldly catapulted itself into a position where it deploys 'soft power'—Al Jazeera, international aid, soon-to-be a Development Fund—a centre of active public diplomacy, summit politics, conference-making, and a conduit of mediatory and dialogical goodwill. Indeed, Al Jazeera satellite TV, with its new style of open and interactive journalism, began a process of rebranding Qatar in the mid-1990s. It embodied an experiment that inducted the region into effective use of soft power. It placed Qatar on the world map, and in the AME this oil-rich Arab state has become associated with a rebirth of pan-Arabism. In particular, from the onset of its coverage of Palestinians under occupation through the occupation of Iraq up to the advent of the Arab uprisings of 2011, an image of Qatar has been solidified in the Arab public opinion as the leading Arab representative of Arab causes. Naturally, this view is contested by some who view Qatar as no more than a Western 'stooge'.

From the programmatic angle, three observations must be made:

(1) Qatar today has moved beyond rebranding its politics: it has now shifted emphasis to *leading*, using the same means of soft power: public diplomacy, international conferences and forums (at the time of writing, Qatar had hosted, starting from 24 September, the week-long 25th Congress of the Universal Postal Union, as well as the Syrian opposition in October 2012 and the 18th United Nations (UN) Climate Change Conference in November 2012), active mediation, active representation of Arab causes (namely, Palestinian) in international forums, global networking through investments (emulating the examples of Singapore and Japan, who invest substantially outside their own national economies), use of international aid (soon to be supplemented with development aid) and Al Jazeera TV. Post-Arab Spring, however, Al Jazeera's role (according to Tunisian scholar, Ezzeddine Abdelmoula, writing a thesis on

satellite TV) is diminishing as a medium as viewers increasingly turn to national media in Egypt, Libya, Tunisia and Yemen.[29]

(2) This trend towards leading is additionally shown in the country's role in upholding the mandate to protect civilians and the 2011 UN Resolution 1973, which eventually led to the ousting of the Gaddafi regime in Libya. Qatar aided the effort not only through Al Jazeera's active coverage and the country's supply of medicine, sales of Libyan petroleum[30] and finance, etc., but also via the logistical support through its own air force and army, which helped train Libyan rebels.[31] This selective use of 'hard power' was executed from above on the basis of a UN mandate. By no means does this act suggest Qatar is re-rebranding itself again. In this instance, Qatar is simply exemplifying its leadership, especially as the US State Secretary called for an active Arab role in Libya. Qatar had the finances, the international bridges and the will to take a lead on this. In deposing Gaddafi, it played perhaps an ad hoc role that projected power far beyond its borders. Libyans welcomed this role.[32] One initiative included a lead role by Qatar to help recover the stolen assets by ousted rulers in Egypt, Libya and Tunisia. Qatar took the lead, hosting the 'Arab Forum on Asset Recovery' opened up by the country's Emir on 11 September 2012 in Doha, to which leaders from the three Arab Spring states and international participants including the UN and the USA were invited.[33] Moreover, Qatar's Attorney General, Ali bin Fetayis Al-Marri, was appointed as the UN legal chief to preside over the stolen asset recovery process.[34]

(3) Qatar's own leadership is somewhat ahead of the learning curve as far as good government is concerned. There appears to be a division of labour, with the Emir-Father, Hamad bin Khalifa Al Thani, being a true visionary: the only monarch to abdicate in favour of his son, Tamim bin Hamad Al Thani. The Emir's advent of power in 1995 was accompanied by gradual induction of reforms: politically, the municipal elections launched in 1999, followed by the 2003 constitution approved through public referendum and officiated as law in 2005. In the 13 May 2015 fifth municipal elections, two women were elected to the Central Municipal Council. Economically, prioritization in the 1990s of gas production over oil proved to be a winner. In the division of labour overseen by the leadership, a kind of pluralist projection of power had been, at the time, gradually and steadily forthcoming, making rule relatively collegiate. This political engine benefited from the partnership to which the country's then Emir lent unfettered support: the visibility and active role played by Shaykha Moza bint Nasser and Prime Minister Shaykh Hamad bin Jassim bin Jaber Al Thani.[35] It is through this leadership network and the hierarchy's division of labour that Qatar's programmatic edge facilitated not only a better coping mechanism with the Arab Spring but also voluntary abdication and a smooth transition of power unprecedented in GCC states. Under the auspices of the then Emir, in November 2008, the country's most ambitious national road map for the realization of a step-up change, making full use of hydrocarbon income was realized: *Qatar National Vision 2030* (*QNV30*). In short, it was a holistic developmental road map, envisioning a take-off along social, political, economic and environmental paths.

In its introduction, *QNV30* states its conceptual framework as capacity building in terms of measuring up to five challenges: equilibrium between the imperatives of modernization and preservation of traditions; fulfilment of the aspiration of current and future generations of Qataris; balancing the demands of socio-economic growth and expansion; wedding need to expatriate quality labour to qualitative development; and putting socio-economic development on an equal footing with environmental protection.[36] In a country where demand for political participation is still modest, not on par with the leadership's eagerness to modernize the political system and upgrade good governance, the development of *QNV30* reflects the country's Emir-demanded inputs from the private sector and society at large. The consultative process, which Qataris themselves know could have benefited from wider participation, was intended to be inclusive. The Emir, time and time again, noted before the country's appointed Advisory Council (*majlas al-shura*) the need for *QNV30* to be a 'shared' programme, involving views from 'the private sector and civil society institutions, [for the purpose of optimizing] full partnership of the [various] components of society'.[37] Qatar's third *National Human Development Report* singles out youth as a target area in need of special attention in a country where half of the population is under the age of 20.[38] This synergetic sequencing gives coherence to *QNV30*: just as the National Development Plan 2011–16 seeks to translate into action the broad outlines embedded within *QNV30*, so does the country's third *Human Development Report*, which partners in the implementation of the plans for human development stated in the 2011–16 strategy.

Qatar can thus be argued to have been a stakeholder in the advent of the Arab Spring, lending support to the Egyptians, Libyans, Syrians and Tunisians to oust dictatorial regimes. The then Prime Minister favoured use of limited 'hard power', short of military intervention, in the resolution of the Syrian uprising as a supplement to soft power. This is despite claims by *Foreign Policy* of Qatar's involvement in funding Jihadists in Syria.[39] The key line of Qatar's policy was to focus on safe havens for civilians and a no-fly zone over Syria.[40] Principally, however, soft power remains the mainstay of Qatar's foreign policy through financing the humanitarian needs of refugees in Turkey and Jordan. In addition, various forums on the uprising, including hosting the Syrian National Council representative of the individuals and groups opposing the authoritarian regime of Bashar Al-Assad, have been sponsored intermittently. The Syrian miasma is not an easy tightrope to walk, and this is one area where results are yet to reveal the massive support invested by Qatar into this version of the Arab Spring in the Levant.

The Orientative/Normative Map

Briefly, Qatar's national development road map, *QNV30*, is underpinned by a normative agenda. This agenda is geared towards serving the four pillars outlined in *QNV30*: human, social, economic and environmental development. Under human development, the ideal of equality is stressed, whereas social development puts forth the principle of a 'just and caring society based on high moral standards'. Elsewhere in *QNV30*, reference is made to the objective to 'protect and promote moral and religious values and traditions'.[41] Shaykhah Moza welcomed the Education High Council's decision the same year to introduce Arabization. She noted Arabization's 'significance for the consolidation of the country's identity'.[42] This normative agenda has also distributive substance: welfarism is part and parcel of Qatar's drive to share income from the petroleum industry. When protests engulfed Arab streets from Tunis to Muscat, the leadership took the bold step of increasing wages by 60 per cent for Qatari citizens, and 120 per cent for the army and police bureaucracies. Whilst cynics viewed the move as a kind of bribe, others especially in Qatar saw it as a step in the right direction through use of further distribution of wealth. Like everywhere in the world, Qatar is not devoid of dissidence, even if this is limited to small pockets of elite scholars and intellectuals wanting a better system of political representation and inclusiveness. However, given the limited or near absent demand by the public at large for political reform, no Arab Spring-like democratization can be expected in Qatar. Finally, the humanitarian dimension gives Qatar's normative agenda a competitive edge, some of which has been palpable in the unfettered support given to the Arab Spring states (finance, medication, increased labour intake and positive publicity in Al Jazeera).

Conclusion

Is there an element of 'mystery' to an oil-rich country using its vast wealth to engage in impact-making foreign policy choices in ways distinguishing it from fellow GCC states? In simple terms, there is none—and definitely conspiratorial thinking such as this, even if present in some discourses, lacks empirically verifiable evidence. Qatar's pursuit of high impact-making policy preferences may be incommensurate with its size, but it can be refigured as totally logical when viewed as being commensurate with its gas riches and high income resulting from the hydrocarbon sector of the economy. Qatar is a country that is remarkable for sticking its neck out for Arab causes, from the besieged Palestinians in Gaza to the impoverished and populous Arab states of the Arab Spring. Investing US\$18 billion in the Egyptian economy[43]— giving the then newly elected post-Mubarak government room for manoeuvre on the economic front—would have raised no eyebrows had the USA done it. Qatar is in a way putting its money where its mouth is: aiding the Arab Spring and closer Arab ties. The Tunisian leadership was promised aid in accordance with higher intake of Tunisian labour:[44] no conspiracy scenarios are yielded from this. Moreover, Qatar is engaging, through its sustained cultivation of a global citizen profile, to help recover, in consortium with the UN, stolen assets from Arab Spring states. However, even soft power has its limits, notwithstanding the best of intentions invested into it. Some policy preferences, especially in the endorsement of Islamists in Libya and Tunisia, have not met with wide popularity. The weak electoral performance by the Islamists may have surprised even Qatar. However, Qatar's involvement in the fight against Gaddafi and the post-Gaddafi order is based on a pragmatic standpoint that diversifies interlocutors and ties. Involvement in Syria, despite the worsening humanitarian situation, violence and absence of success, has not dissuaded Qatar from continuing its support for the Friends of Syria Forum, its endorsement of Syrian opposition and financial aid to Syrian refugees. Most importantly, its involvement, which cannot be assumed to be motivated by profit since Qatar is a vastly rich country,[45] has created a niche. Where GCC states have taken a back seat in the running of Arab–Arab relations, Qatar has built kudos and leadership credentials that surpass its size and relatively short history of involvement in pan-Arab affairs.

What raises eyebrows is the 'intrepid' diversification evidenced by having at once one of the largest US bases in the world aiding Hamas and not precluding, for instance, conducting communication, even if low key, with Israel. The US base has given the Qatari leadership breathing space, relatively overcoming the kind of insecurity found in most GCC states. The Al-Udeid US airbase, south of Doha with its new radar facilities, must be a source of comfort for other GCC states. The responsibility is Qatari but the benefit is really more shared, and even the Saudis must draw at least psychological dividend from its propinquity. Maybe it is partly Qatar's ability to put the security question to bed that is helping it get on with the job of making waves economically and diplomatically. Qatar today is banking on its success in rebranding itself through soft power, especially Al Jazeera TV, international forums, expatriate labour, development aid, international sports (2011 Asian Cup) and global economic investments. It is the dividends from that rebranding that are today informing its current shift or upgrade of its policy choices into leadership. This has been most evident in the lead role played by Qatar in the Arab Spring. There is much evidence of change, thus going against the gist of suggestions that monarchical exceptionalism inhibits the change of Gulf States in the context of the Arab Spring. One conclusion from this is that the GCC is not a monolith, and change takes diverse forms and permutations.

Disclosure Statement

No potential conflict of interest was reported by the author.

Notes

[1] Dina Shehata, 'The fall of the Pharaoh: how Hosni Mubarak's regime came to an end', *Foreign Affairs*, 90, May–June 2011, pp. 26–32.

[2] Fouad Ajami, 'Five myths about the Arab Spring', *Washington Post*, 12 January 2012, < http://www.washingtonpost.com/opinions/five-myths-about-the-arab-spring/2011/12/21/gIQA32TVuP_story.html> (accessed 18 April 2015).

[3] Nazih Ayubi, *Over-stating the Arab State: Politics and Society in the Middle East*, I. B. Tauris, London, 1995.

[4] Hamid Dabashi, *The Arab Spring: The End of Postcolonialism*, Zed Books, London, 2012.

[5] Samuel P. Huntington, *The Third Wave: Democratisation in the Late Twentieth Century*, University of Oklahoma Press, Norman, 1991.

[6] It is succinctly defined here as forms of exclusionary power that happen under either secular or traditional rule across the Arab geography; and is additionally noted for near or total absence of competitive, representative and accountable politics. Moreover, when elections take place as was the case in countries such as Egypt, Tunisia and Yemen before the 2011 ousters, they did not result in democratic government. This notion is described as a form of 'electoral fetishism'. See Larbi Sadiki, *Rethinking Arab Democratization: Elections without Democracy*, Oxford University Press, Oxford, 2009.

[7] Michael Herb, *All in the Family: Revolution, Absolutism and Democracy in Middle East Monarchies*, SUNY Press, Albany, 1999.

[8] Harold D. Lasswell, *Politics: Who Gets What, When, How*, Whittlesey House McGraw-Hill Book Company, London, 1936.

[9] See Robert Michels, *Political Parties: A Sociological Study of the Oligarchical Tendencies of Modern Democracies*, Batoche Books, Kitchener, Ontario, 2001.

[10] John D. May, 'Democracy, organization, Michels', *American Political Science Review*, 59(2), June 1965, pp. 417–429.

[11] Huntington, op. cit., pp. 1–30.

[12] Gabriel Almond and Sydney Verba, *The Civic Culture: Political Attitudes and Democracy in Five Nations*, Little, Brown, Boston, 1965.

[13] Benedict Anderson, *Imagined Communities*, Verso, London, 2006.

[14] Ibid., p. 6.

[15] Ibid.

[16] Ibid., p. 7.

[17] Ibid., p. 7. Anderson states: 'Coming to maturity at a stage of human history when even the most devout adherents of any universal religion were inescapably confronted with the living pluralism of such religions, and the allomorphism between each faith's ontological claims and territorial stretch, nations dream of being free, and, if, under God, directly so. The gage and emblem of this freedom is the sovereign state.'

[18] Ibid., p. 7.

[19] Eric Hobsbawm, *The Age of Revolutions, 1789–1884*, Abacus, London, 1962; Eric Hobsbawm, *The Age of Extremes: A History of the World, 1914–1991*, Michael Joseph, London, 1994.

[20] The celebrated Lebanese-American author, Nassim Taleb, considers Saudi Arabia to be the most fragile country in the world. Nassim Taleb, *Anti-fragile: How to Live in a World We Don't Understand*, Vol. 3, Allen Lane, New York, 2012.

[21] See 'Qatar court upholds poet's jail sentence', *Al Jazeera*, 21 October 2013, <http://www.aljazeera.com/news/middleeast/2013/10/qatar-court-upholds-sentence-against-poet-20131021123723850815.html> (accessed 20 April 2015).

[22] Ulf Laessing, 'Saudi king back home, orders $37 billion handouts', *Reuters*, 23 February 2011.

[23] Edwar Edward, *Orientalism: Western Conceptions of the Orient*, Penguin Books, London, 1978; Timothy Mitchell, *Colonising Egypt*, Cambridge University Press, Cambridge, 1988.

[24] Lisa Anderson, 'Absolutism and the resilience of monarchy in the Middle East', *Political Science Quarterly*, 106(2), 1991, pp. 1–15.

[25] Russell Lucas, 'Monarchical authoritarianism: survival and political liberalization in a Middle Eastern regime type', *International Journal of Middle East Studies*, 36(1), 2004, pp. 103–119.

[26] Sean Yom and F. Gregory Gause III, 'Resilient royals: how Arab monarchies hang on', *Journal of Democracy*, 23(4), October 2012, pp. 74–88.

[27] Ibid., p. 75.

[28] Mehran Kamrava, *Qatar: Small State, Big Politics*, Cornell University Press, Ithaca, NY, 2013, p. 68.

[29] Author interview, Ezzeddine Abdelmoula, Jazeera Studies Centre, Doha, 3 October 2012.

[30] According to an article in the *Gulf Times*, this involved Qatar's supply of four shipments of petroleum to the Port of Benghazi and sale of two out of the Port of Tobruk. See 'Emir receives head of Libyan National Panel', *Gulf Times*, 19 April 2011, <http://www.gulftimes.com/site/topics/article.asp?cu_no=2&item_no = 429284&version = 1&template_id = 36&parent_id = 16 > (accessed 12 October 2012).

[31] Michael Buchanan, 'Qatar flexing muscle in changing world', *BBC News*, 28 December 2011, <http://www.bbc.co.uk/news/world-middle-east-16348250?print=true > (accessed 14 October 2012).

[32] The then head of Libya's National Transitional Council, Mustafa Abd Al-Jalil, thanked Qatar whilst on an official visit to Doha. See 'Emir receives head of Libyan National Panel', *Gulf Times*,

19 April 2011, < http://www.gulftimes.com/site/topics/article.asp?cu_no=2&item_no = 429284&version = 1&template_id = 36&parent_id = 16 > (accessed 12 October 2012).

[33] Ramesh Matthew, 'Call to recover stolen assets', *Gulf Times*, 12 September 2012, < http://www. gulf-times.com/site/topics/printArticle.asp?cu_no=2&item_no = 530732&version = 1& template_id = 57&parent_id = 56 > (accessed 10 October 2012).

[34] Wafa Zayid, 'Qatar Muhamiyan li Al-Shu'ub al-Madlumah' [Qatar, advocate of wronged peoples], *Al-Sharq*, Doha, 2 September 2012.

[35] Shaykhah Moza's father, Nasser Al Misnad, was one of the leading civil society activists who took a lead in the call for equality for Qatar citizens in the early and mid-1960s when Britain was running Qatar. He passed away in 2007.

[36] See *Qatar National Vision 2030*, General Secretariat for Development, Doha, 2008.

[37] See Emir Hamad bin Khalifa Al Tahni's speeches.

[38] *Qatar National Human Development Report*, State of Qatar, Doha, 2012.

[39] Elizabeth Dickinson, 'The case against Qatar', *Foreign Policy*, 30 September 2014, < http:// www.foreignpolicy.com/articles/2014/09/30/the_case_against_qatar_funding_extremists_ salafi_syria_uae_jihad_muslim_brotherhood_taliban> (accessed 2 December 2014).

[40] Confirmed on Foreign Ministry's Homepage: see 'Premier denies Qatar sends weapons to Syria', 19 October 2012, < http://english.mofa.gov.qa/newsPage.cfm?newsid=22951 > (accessed 19 October 2012).

[41] *Qatar National Vision 2030*, op. cit., pp. 5–6.

[42] For further details, see 'Her Highness Shaykhah Moza visits Qatar University', in QU's magazine, *Campus Life*, Second term 2012, p. 6.

[43] 'Qatar Tastathmiru 18 Milyar Dolar fi Misr' [Qatar invests 18 billion dollars in Egypt], *Al-Ra'yah*, Doha, 7 September 2012, pp. 1–3.

[44] According to talks by the author with Tunisian advisors and leaders. The promises were made to both Rachid Ghannouhci and President Moncef Marzouki, and implementation is underway, with thousands of Tunisians (applies equally to Egyptians amongst other Arabs) having already joined the Qatari labour market.

[45] According to reports related to Mustafa Abd Al-Jalil, Qatar invested nearly US$1 billion in aiding the Libyan revolution, see Joelle El-Khoury (trans.), 'Qatar sends billions, hoping for an Islamic regime in Libya', *Al Monitor*, 3 August 2012, < http://www.al-monitor.com/pulse/security/01/ 08/report-warns-about-a-serious-thr.html#ixzz29kvxya74> (accessed 1 October 2012).

Larbi Sadiki is an Australian-Tunisian scholar of Middle East politics. He specializes in the study of Arab democratic transitions. He is the editor of *Routledge Handbook of the Arab Spring* (London, 2015) and the editor of the series *Routledge Studies in Middle Eastern Democratization and Government* (http://www.routledge.com/books/ series/RSMEDG/). He writes for Al Jazeera English and is currently based in Doha, where he is Associate Professor of international affairs at Qatar University.

Turkey and Iran: The Two Modes of Engagement in the Middle East

E. Fuat Keyman and Onur Sazak

A series of breakthroughs in Iran's contentious affairs with the West necessitate a new way of thinking on Turkey–Iran relations. Hassan Rouhani's victory in the 2013 Iranian presidential elections and the signing of the interim Geneva nuclear agreement between Iran and the 'P5 + 1' shortly thereafter warrant an overhaul of the conventional policies concerning the Islamic Republic. Coupled with the Arab uprisings, recent developments will significantly impact not only the way Turkey and Iran approach each other but also their regional policies. This paper seeks to shed light on the two different modes of engagement that Turkey and Iran have employed vis-à-vis their approach to their shared neighbourhood. That is, while Turkey is positioned to utilize this breakthrough on a global scale to improve its relations with Iran and other countries through 'humanitarian diplomacy'; on the regional level, Tehran's hegemonic and interest-based ambitions will stoke the subtle rivalry with Ankara. This paper provides a background for the origins of these two different modes of engagement and discusses how they have influenced the dynamics in the region. After pointing out how the recent developments concerning Iran's nuclear programme and engagement in certain regional conflicts shape the Ankara–Tehran dialogue, it concludes with the implications of these competitive approaches for the greater Middle East.

Introduction

The much-needed silver lining in Iran's stormy relations with the West appeared with the 2013 presidential elections. The reform-minded candidate Hassan Rouhani's landslide victory has tipped the scales in favour of a possible normalization in both the domestic politics and foreign policy of Iran. Shortly after Rouhani's coming to power, Iran signed the interim nuclear agreement in Geneva with the USA, the UK, France, Russia, China and Germany (collectively referred to as 'P5 + 1'). The deal would suspend certain aspects of Iran's nuclear activity that would produce nuclear weapons in exchange for economic relief. A little over a year after this development, the negotiations in Lausanne in March and April 2015 yielded another window of opportunity for a more durable normalization between Iran and the rest. The Joint Comprehensive Plan of Action (JCPOA), a communiqué that emerged from the 2 April 2015 convention, lays the terms of the

West's progressive engagement in return for a significant reduction in Iran's capacity to develop nuclear weapons.[1]

These developments forewarn an imminent change in conventional thinking, strategies and policies on Iran. Furthermore, they are destined to affect Turkey's relationship with Iran. The relations between the two countries had already been turbulent by the 2013 elections. The eruption of the so-called 'Arab Spring' and its spillover to Turkey and Iran's near neighbourhood had triggered a subtle rivalry between the two actors to institute their contrasting visions for the future of the region. In light of each actor's aspiration for regional leadership, and the rooted competition between the two to achieve it, this is hardly unanticipated. After all, when one studies the history of Turkish–Iranian relations, one notices a fluctuating relationship where relatively smaller intervals of honeymoon periods are followed by long periods of skirmishes and hostile attitudes.

A subtle point that one must acknowledge to better grasp the Turkey–Iran dynamic is the shared post-imperial characteristics, yet different political evolutions, of the two nations: both are post-imperial social formations, strong nation-states, republics and regional pivots. However, each has evolved differently. While Turkey embarked on democratization and modernization under Mustafa Kemal Atatürk's guidance, Iran was ruled under totalitarian regimes and decayed further into isolation and authoritarianism. Turkey has emerged extroverted and engaged with the world through its own experimentation with democracy and modernity. Iran, on the other hand, especially in the aftermath of the 1979 revolution, was cast out of the international community and tethered its survival to hegemonic aspirations for its neighbourhood. In brief, certain convergences, or rather more defining divergences, have shaped Turkey and Iran's unique modes of engagement with the region.

The prospect of Iran's gradual opening up to the world even changes the dynamics of the turbulent relationship between Turkey and Iran. Amid these new developments, we predict the two modes of engagement that Turkey and Iran will seek to influence the future of their regions. First, taking advantage of the positive atmosphere of increased humanitarian aid on the global scale, Turkey will continue to pursue a constructive humanitarian diplomacy that puts institutional and economic development of its neighbours first. On the regional level, however, Iran's determination to realize its hegemonic ambitions and security- and interest-driven foreign policy in the region is expected to fuel the rivalry between the two regional powerhouses. Worse, the deteriorating conditions in Syria and Yemen, coupled with Turkey and Iran's conflicting modes of engagement with these countries, may fuel a proxy war. The paper therefore seeks to explain Turkey's mode of engagement and policies on the stability and development of its neighbourhood first. Then, we compare it with Iran's approach and therefore pinpoint the key differences. We will next elaborate on two recent vital developments that may play a considerable role in the competition and rift between Turkey and Iran in the long run: Iran's nuclear ambitions and the security measures that Turkey has taken against the increasing tension in the region. The conclusion will present a number of forecasts regarding the direction of relations between the two countries and whether the two modes of engagement will endure.

Turkey in the Middle East: A New Era of 'Zero Problems'

In his *Foreign Policy* article, then Foreign Minister and current Prime Minister Ahmet Davutoğlu indicates that the effects of the original zero problems approach are about to come to maturation.[2] In other words, as the new governments that came with uprisings take root in the region, and as Turkey builds bridges with these administrations and revitalizes its old, prosperous relations with some of its traditional allies, the number of countries that Turkey enjoys steady relations with will eventually surpass those with which the relations are still uncertain. In fact, the countries that opt out of a progressive and peaceful relationship are likely to be at a disadvantage in light of the recent developments.

The six major tenets of Turkish foreign policy that Davutoğlu stresses explain the steadfast posture that Turkey can afford to take in its neighbourhood: a balance between security and freedom, zero problems with neighbours, a multidimensional foreign policy, a proactive regional foreign policy, an altogether new diplomatic style and rhythmic diplomacy.[3] To understand what sets apart Turkish foreign policy from that of others in the region, one must first comprehend the fine balance between security, self-interest and freedom that Ankara underscores. Davutoğlu explains this balance very clearly. He asserts that as far as Turkey's engagement with a country or region is concerned, at the core of its relationship always lie ethics, morals and commitment to freedom. And secondary to these values are security and economic and political self-interest, all of which can be summed under realpolitik.[4] Turkey, therefore, works carefully and tirelessly to aid those countries with a value and ethics-based approach, while maintaining the balance between security and freedom.

With its ability to sustain, and even deepen, its secular democracy in a peaceful manner, along with its 'dual identity as both a Middle Eastern and European country', Turkey's recent governance by the Justice and Development Party (AKP) and its electoral victories, as well as its proactive foreign policy engagements, have made Turkey a 'pivotal state and regional power' in an uncertain, risky, insecure and rapidly globalizing world. Turkey is the only country that can talk to both the West and the rest, to the Western leaders and the Middle Eastern leaders, and to the North and the South. While going through the full accession negotiations with the European Union (EU), Turkey's regional and global engagements have been widening and deepening. Turkey's Europeanization, on the one hand, and its regional engagements with the Middle East, the Balkans and Caucasus, as well as with Africa and the Muslim world, on the other hand, have been dually unfolding. In responding to the current global financial and political instability, Turkey has actively initiated a number of multilayered engagements.

Turkey's past experience and connection with the West as a steadfast eastern bulwark against the Soviet threat, the reliability and trustworthiness that it gained from the West during this era, and a mild identity crisis that it experienced with the collapse of the Soviet Union until the early 2000s and through to the post-9/11 world had a role to play in all of this. With initiatives from the late President Turgut Özal and then Foreign Minister İsmail Cem, Turkey tried to steer out of this identity crisis with a multilayered and multilateral foreign policy. This new foreign policy mindset was nurtured with a certain degree of discontinuity. Most importantly, this new approach, vested largely in bilateral relations rather than alliances or regional blocs, set the course for the systematic implementation of the effective post-9/11 policies that were mentioned earlier.

With its successful economic performance, supported by a young and economically dynamic population, its capacity to adapt globalization and Europeanization, and its increasing regional and global economic engagements, Turkey's active globalization and proactive foreign policy has fostered its transformation into a 'trading state'.[5] During the 2000s, Turkey's economic growth rate has been high, Turkey's commercial activities have widened regionally and globally, including in new geographies such as Africa and the Middle East. Furthermore, Turkey has become an important player in international organizations such as the G-20. Turkey has become one of the important, but not pivotal (such as India and Brazil), 'emerging market economies' of today's economic globalization. To ensure the success of its trading state identity, Turkey has dropped its visa requirements with an increasing number of countries and attempted to enhance its economic and cultural engagements and dialogue interactions with them. Turkey has made use of the global context for its benefit and has attempted to globalize its trading state identity, including the regions of Africa and Latin America. The economic dynamism of Turkey has drawn a growing global interest and attraction.[6]

In the deepening of Turkey–EU relations and the beginning of full accession negotiations, there was an increasing perception, especially among economic and foreign policy actors, that Turkey was a 'unique case in the process of European integration' with the ability to help Europe to become a multicultural and cosmopolitan model for a deep regional integration. From this point of view, Turkey could be the driver of a post-territorial community on the basis of post-national and democratic citizenship, and also a global actor with a capacity to contribute to the emergence of democratic global governance. The possibility of Europe gaining these qualities depends to some extent on its decision about the accession of Turkey in the EU as a full member.[7]

As of late, humanitarian intervention and assistance has become one of the central concerns of international relations amidst the global turmoil driven by transnational security concerns, bleak economic outlook and rapid environmental degradation. With its soft power, while emerging as a proactive actor in foreign policy, Turkey has also been a regional and global force in peacekeeping and humanitarian operations. It has become one of the key 'global humanitarian actors of world politics'.[8] Turkey has increasingly been involved in humanitarian assistance in different regions of the world. In doing so it is not only contributing to global security but also strengthening new 'human-based' norms of democratic global governance. Turkey's civilian humanitarian aid to the Palestinians in Gaza, its involvement in Afghanistan, its peacekeeping contributions in different parts of the world and its recent engagement in Africa in general, and in Somalia and Sudan in particular, have demonstrated Turkey's increasing global humanitarian state role and identity in global affairs. These initiatives have also concurred Turkey's multilateral engagements to propagate humanitarian practices as vital instruments of diplomacy to make globalization fair and humane.[9]

These examples sum up an axiom about Turkey's foreign policy, and they set it apart from the others. That is, Turkey does not necessarily want to be a model for the region. It respects the sovereignty of its neighbours. Ankara does not have an agenda to impose its own democratization or institutionalization processes on others. Rather the Turkish government acknowledges that some of the policies it has followed for the last few decades expedited its development pace and produced tangible economic growth and welfare for the majority of Turkish citizens. The pioneers of this growth-based development are confident that similar policies and initiatives can replicate such favourable outcomes in the countries that wish to emulate them.

Furthermore, since the beginning of the Arab uprisings, the Turkish government has communicated clearly that it has no desire, or a grand design, to get involved in nation building in these countries. Nonetheless, it has committed its structural help through advanced economic and commercial relations with these countries. Ankara remains adamant in using its soft power to inspire these nations to achieve the same level of economic development that it has reached and sustained.[10]

One must also take into account that the Turkish model is unique. Its adaptation by the incipient Arab movements may not yield the same institutions of Turkish democracy. Turkey's experience with secularism and laicism is endogenous to Turkey's own reformation process since the early 1920s. Its democratization has been significantly influenced by efforts to reconcile power within the military establishment with democracy and a secular system with religious orientation. This constructive contention has also served as a model of economic success and a workable culture between the East and West in the Turkish case.

In the same vein, the Arab uprising countries are reluctant to accept the Turkish model per se. The Turkish model is still viewed as the model of the outsider, incompatible with the realities and peculiarities of the region. The majority of the Arab revolutionaries see the model debate through the prism of the Ottoman legacy in the Middle East. Certain countries, like Egypt, may feel indifferent toward, even appreciative of, this legacy. Moreover, most actors of the Arab uprisings recognize the destabilizing legacy of the Turkish military on the democratization process in Turkey. Given the victories in Tunisia and Libya against authoritarian regimes, and the ongoing contest for power between the Egyptian public and the military custodians of the government, the last thing these movements want is a democratization process that is 'assisted' by the military. It should be pointed out, however, that if Turkey approaches the Arab uprisings not unilaterally but in coordination and collaboration with the EU, and by presenting itself not only as a dynamic and transforming country but also as a country moving towards EU full membership status, then, both its contribution to the process of the transition to democracy in this region and the perception of such contribution by the peoples and the governments of these countries could increase and widen.

In fact, Turkey can still provide substantive assistance to the democratization process in its neighbourhood. In this regard, Turkey's most significant contribution will be to share its best practices in sustainable economic development. In both areas,

Turkey–EU cooperation is crucial. Over the last decade, Turkey has transformed its private sector, made its markets more transparent and competitive, and instated necessary financial and market regulations to increase the confidence of foreign investors. By the same token, the state has undertaken effective reforms to strengthen its social services. Today, the quality of health care and access to education services are almost incomparable to the 1990s and 1980s in terms of the progress made in each sector.

Based on this experience, Turkey can introduce effective solutions to some of the current economic ills of the Arab uprising countries. As the former head of the United Nations Development Program (UNDP) Kemal Derviş suggests, the Arab uprising countries need policies that eradicate the rent-seeking capitalism or reliance on discredited state bureaucracy.[11] More important, 'a truly competitive private sector has to be unleashed' and 'neither the old statist left, nor the rent-seeking, crony capitalist right had policies to respond' to this need.[12] In this respect, Turkey can use both its expertise with the free markets that have been developing significantly since the 1980s and the responsible growth era of the last decade, to guide the Arab uprising countries. In fact, it is in the areas of economy and democracy that the contribution of Turkey to the Arab uprisings mainly lies.

Iran's Middle East Policy and Divergences with Turkey in Regional Perspectives

Iran's regional policy, as well as its foreign policy at large, has three central tenets: first, Tehran favours the preservation of the status quo in the Middle East and North Africa (MENA);[13] second, the Iranian regime wants to export its religious revolution to the neighbouring countries;[14] third, Tehran desires to protect the Shiite regimes in its immediate vicinity and position them as proxies.[15] Iran's first objective greatly contradicts the current trends emerging in the region. While Tehran is concerned about the ripple effect of the liberation movements going all around its vicinity, for all the predictable reasons, the readout of the situation does not signal an immediate end to this sweep of reforms. Bülent Aras, the former head of the Turkish Foreign Ministry's Strategic Research Center (SAM), articulates this point in his policy analysis, entitled 'Turkey and Iran: Facing the Challenge of the Arab Spring'. Aras advances that the recent mass demonstrations and civil strife in the MENA region were not only geared towards the provision of fundamental rights, but they also represented a new perspective on 'ethical perspectives in a changing international system, with the relative decline of former hegemonic powers and the rise of new countries'.[16] He further depicts this massive transition as 'a serious blow to the Middle East's *status quo*'.

> The former models of inward-oriented rulers, who were resistant to international influences, are giving way to new outward-looking leaders with a focus on honor, liberty, freedom, and good governance. The Arab uprisings have also challenged the survival strategies of authoritarian rules through changes in regional power balances, international alliances, and an emulation of Asian developmentalist models.[17]

Aras' analysis of the situation reveals the imperative defining factors behind Iran's resilient attachment to the crumbling status quo and support for the elements that defend the other. In fact, Iran has tried a mix of strategies and introduced different conceptual definitions of this new phenomenon to deflect the Arab uprisings' spillover effects from its own society and the others that are governed by repressive regimes and minority political dynasties. For instance, Tehran first welcomed the uprisings in the Arab countries shortly after their breakout. Mainly the clergy[18] either misconstrued or rhetorically manipulated them as anti-Western and pro-Islamic movements. They drew parallels between the 1979 Iranian revolution and today's demonstrations and referred to the perpetrators as 'ideological allies'.[19] For them, the power balance in the region was in favour of Iran's dominance. Increasing the power and influence of Iran would lead to a sharp decline of US dominance in the region. In other words, Iran regarded this first phase of the uprisings as an Islamic awakening and dreamed of a region that is ruled under Islamic rule. With the eruption of demonstrations in Syria, as well as the first signs of their potential escalation into a civil war, Iran perceived the movement within Syria as a serious threat against its interest in the region, particularly to Tehran's Alewite allies in Damascus. The political change of heart in Tehran was soon reflected in the rhetorical shift in the messages sent to the globe by the Islamic Republic. This time, in the Iranian government's eyes, it was the West that sowed the seeds of the revolution and exacerbated them. In other words, Western security and economic interests were behind the events blazing through the MENA region to create a power balance in the region that would tilt outcomes in the West's favour.[20]

With these principles legitimized by the Iranian constitution and supposedly instilled in the Iranian foreign policy, there emerges an intrinsic conundrum between principle and practice, which would be difficult to address in light of Iran's current foreign policy practices. Retrospectively, Iran today is not only far from standing up to hegemons in the region (if we set aside the Iranian President Ahmadinejad's frequent rhetorical outbursts at Israel and the USA), but it rather chooses to be their ally. In addition to standing by the oppressed, as sanctioned by its constitution, Tehran commits its resources to building defences around those who commit atrocities against their fellow Muslims. Şahin underlines that:

> Iran's foreign policy is undergoing a new test with the Arab uprisings in the region. In this process, while Iran supports opposition groups in some countries like Bahrain and Yemen when thinking of its own interests, it cozies up to the authoritarian and secular government in some countries such as Syria.[21]

Therefore, it baffles Şahin that while the Iranian constitution necessitates that the regime should stand by the oppressed, just as in the 1982 invasion of Lebanon, Tehran 'does not see any mistake in supporting the oppressors responsible for the massacres occurring in Syria'.[22] Aras notes the same irony. The Turkish scholar said:

The Iranian establishment tried to claim some success in the uprisings by framing it as Islamic awakening. This is also an attempt to play to a domestic audience and preserve their hold on power at home. Their aim is simply regime maintenance and survival.[23]

When we dig deeper into this mismatch between the Iranian rhetoric and policy action, we notice the third remaining constant of the Iranian foreign policy: the defence and preservation of the Shiite regimes in the neighbourhood. Iran is not shy about showing its support for the Shiite regimes in the region. It waged proxy wars in Lebanon first, following its invasion by Israeli forces in 1982. Iran's continuing support for the Hezbollah elements in the Lebanese government is one of the biggest open secrets in the region. During the short war between Israel and the Hezbollah elements in Lebanon in 2006, the latter relied on the Iranian logistical and military support to stand firm against a technologically and tactically advanced Israeli army. In the same vein, students of Middle Eastern politics observe a significant change in Iran's policy vis-à-vis Iraq. In the aftermath of the US invasion of Iraq, Tehran actively pursued a proxy war to create a sphere of influence over the Shiite majority. The clerics' objective was to ensure and support an overwhelming Shiite participation in the new Iraqi government and Shiite presence in the ranks of the new decision-making schema.[24] Iran also carefully stirred the regions where Shiites were a minority and featured strongholds of dominant groups. One such region is Northern Iraq, run by the Kurdish majority. Immediately after the invasion, Iranian paramilitary forces and intelligence contested rigorously to create a sphere of influence by recruiting the Islamic Movement of Iraqi Kurdistan.[25]

In summary, the three drivers of Iran's foreign policy goals can be vaguely identified as self-survival through the maintenance of the status quo in the MENA region, exportation of the religious themes of the old revolution, and protection of its interests and influence over the region by defending its Shiite allies. As the earlier illustrations have shown, reaching these objectives comes at a great ethical and credibility cost of the regime in Tehran. To ensure its survival, Iran visibly goes against the founding principles of its regime. But more importantly, Iran's reckless attitude against the vital developments sweeping the region hurts its relations with reliable partners the most. Turkey being one of them.

The General Trends and Current Strains in Turkish–Iranian Relations

A roller-coaster ride is a proper metaphor for alluding to the last two decades of Turkish–Iranian relations. From the early 1990s to date, the nature of the relationship shifted from suspicion and mistrust to cooperation and solidarity, and recently back to a state of caution and conflicting interests. Security has always been at the forefront of the relations and is seconded by commercial and cultural engagements. However, both countries make strange bedfellows at best given their uncanny similarities and differences. Both Turkey and Iran are post-imperial social formations. Each comes from a strong state tradition and practised state-centric modernity. Each modernity project imposed a top-down transformation of society. Security and nationalism were key drivers of modernity in Turkey. Under Mustafa Kemal Atatürk's vision, Turkey had to follow a Western-oriented foreign policy and domestic modernization agenda in order to obtain security, for the latter was very much related to catching up with the technological and societal advancements of Europe in order not to repeat the demise of the Ottoman Empire. Similarly, Iran also used nationalism and state-powered realist policies to reinforce its revolution. Iran was also pragmatic in terms of catching up with various Western technology (such as nuclear reactors and defence systems) to better consolidate its position in the world. However, one big difference between the two countries was always Turkey's extroverted international personality, whereas Iran closed its gates to the world after the revolution and isolated itself in a theologically and nationalistically construed bubble. Turkey has always been engaged with the world and has never forsaken the fundamental principles of democracy and secularism. Iran, on the other hand, more so after the revolution, cared less for these principles and valued more the tenets of a totalitarian and theocratic regime.

Normalization of the relations came in late 2002 when US intentions to invade Iraq were as clear as daylight. Realizing the potential of an independent Kurdish state rising in the midst of an approaching chaos, Iran, Turkey and Syria held conventions to develop strategies that would contain such an outcome. Ironically, a similar meeting was suggested at yet another Economic Cooperation Organization (ECO) summit—this time organized in Turkey. Then Iranian President Khatami was extremely vocal about the need to form some sort of a coalition between the three countries against a possible independent Kurdish state in Northern Iraq and the implications of such a state for their respective countries. Khatami objected to a unified Kurdish administration in the region. He was especially worried about the function of this prospective state in the instance of an Israeli attack on Iran. A Kurdish state bordering Iran would serve as an ideal bulwark, or an outpost, facilitating Israeli campaigns into the Iranian territory.

This period of normalization coincided with the rise of the AKP in Turkey. The dialogue mentioned above increased during the early hours of the AKP administration. In a number of ensuing 'Neighbors of Iraq' conferences both the AKP administration and its counterparts in Iran recognized the emergence of an independent Kurdish state on the flanks of their sovereign territories and pledged cooperation against it.

With the AKP in office, the paradigms that fuelled the subtle rivalry between the two countries shifted. Tehran, on the one hand, no longer had to deal with a secularist elite as its counterpart in Turkey. Ankara, on the other, no more concerned itself with questioning the regime in Iran. This was dramatically different from how the relations between the two governments had played out in the late 1990s. Turkish governments at the time would make deliberate congratulatory statements on the electoral victories of progressive and reformist factions of the Islamist regime. Tehran, in effect, would perceive these statements as direct interference with Iran's domestic politics. By the same token, Turkey would relate the activities of rogue and violent proxies such as Turkish Hezbollah to the Iranian government's ambition to tamper with the secular and relatively democratic regime in Turkey. These suspicions disappeared with the advent of the AKP, and the relations took a positive turn.

From 2004 to spring 2011, the Turkish–Iranian relations were on a steady incline, in spite of minor disagreements. The first subtle support for the Iranian regime from Ankara came during the 2005 elections. President Ahmadinejad's victory at the ballots instigated a fervent disapproval among the Western powers due to Ahmadinejad's radical tendencies vis-à-vis Israel, ultra-conservative policies and open animosity towards the Western institutions and influence. Turkish officials, staying on the outside of this camp, did not issue any concerns; they rather commented that the elections were part of Iran's domestic business and did not concern external actors. Similarly, when Ahmadinejad won the re-elections in 2009, which were rigged and corrupted, Turkish President Abdullah Gül was the first one to congratulate him in spite of the evidence indicating the fraud and mass protests against the re-elected president, which resulted in serious civilian casualties, unwarranted arrests and major human rights violations.

In this era, Turkey became perhaps the most ardent supporter of Iran's nuclear programme. From 2006 onward, the Turkish government tried to mediate the differences between the Islamic Republic and P5 + 1. Prime Minister Erdoğan personally vouched for the peaceful nature of Iran's nuclear programme. Touring the Western capitals until 2010, Erdoğan called on the major powers plus Israel to decrease their nuclear arsenal before stifling Iran's nuclear ambitions. In late 2009 and early 2010, Turkey and Brazil attempted to broker an agreement between Iran and P5 + 1 on the former nuclear enrichment programme. The proposal suggested that Iran would send its low-enriched uranium to an agreed state, or multiple states, and these states would supply Iran with higher quality uranium rods as fuel. The proposal was killed in the United Nations (UN) General Assembly in May 2010, and the Permanent Members of the Security Council arguing that this deal would still leave Iran with enough low-grade uranium to be enriched into weapon-grade plutonium.

The constructive relations between the two countries have tumbled in a downward spiral since the spread of the Arab uprisings to a more immediate region encircling Syria. The way Turkey and Iran have responded to the Syrian crisis is illustrative of each country's approach to the Arab uprisings. Infuriated by the atrocities of the Assad regime, Turkey first adamantly called for an end to the violent crackdown of the government forces on the dissidents. With the escalation of the civil unrest into a civil war, Ankara cut its relations with Damascus completely and opened the channels of humanitarian aid for the internally displaced Syrians. Today, over 2 million Syrian refugees reside in Turkey; they are mostly concentrated in adjacent provinces of south-eastern Turkey, waiting out the bloody war unfolding next door. Ankara, in the meantime, confers with its NATO (North Atlantic Treaty Organization) and European allies on the feasibility of a humanitarian corridor maintained and secured by an international coalition. Although a direct military intervention lacks unanimous support among Turkey's allies, Ankara nonetheless holds tightly to the idea of Assad's removal as the only viable outcome of the turmoil in Syria.

Iran, by contrast, chimes in with Russia and China and opposes any type of military intervention in Syria. Tehran does not waver from its original stance and reiterates that the civil war in Syria is a domestic affair and is off-limits to foreign intervention. Iran's backing of the Assad regime is consistent with its general policy to support status quos in the countries swept by the uprisings. However, it is worth emphasizing that Iran's siding with the great powers of Russia and China raises a new challenge for Turkey, namely, one of nuclear security.

Syria and Yemen as Catalysts for Iran's Hegemonic Ambitions

The unravelling of Syria appears to have motivated Iran to declare its hegemonic aspirations in an unusual and increasing candour. Ali Younesi, a senior advisor to the Iranian President Rouhani, has recently confirmed Iran's greater vision of becoming a hegemon—in other words an empire.[26] Younesi, the head of intelligence of the former President Khatami, has stated that 'since its inception Iran has always had a global dimension'.[27] According to Younesi, Iran will eventually realize its original boundaries and seize its natural territories, which spans a vast territory from the borders of China (including the Indian subcontinent as well as Central Asia) to the north and south basins of the Persian Gulf.[28] Younesi has also issued an open challenge to Saudi Arabia by rendering the latter's dedication to the protection of Muslims invalid. The former head of intelligence has vouched not only that Iran can defend the interests of Muslims better but also that the Iran–Shiite version of Islam is the pure version of Islam.[29]

In tandem with the Iranian government's bold rhetoric, the fledgling security situation in Syria and the escalation of tensions in Yemen constitute the basis of a new alliance among Turkey, Saudi Arabia and Qatar. Iran's advance in both countries has driven Ankara and Riyadh to align their objectives vis-à-vis Syria. It has been frequently reported over the last several weeks that Turkey supports the Saudi operations in Yemen and that both countries actively equip and train Syrian opposition forces (with particular emphasis on Jaish al-Fatah [the Army of Conquest] which comprises of insurgent groups such as al-Nusrah, the al-Qaeda franchise in Syria).[30]

This increased schism between Iran and Turkey over regional priorities risks a proxy war. In fact, experts in the region speak of multiple proxy wars between Iran and various actors. One scenario that centres on Syria juxtaposes Iran and Turkey as main rivals in this proxy war and projects that each country is trying hard to penetrate into the other's sphere of influence. The proponents of this view claim that Iran uses the Kurdish insurgents to cause instability within Turkey, and by these means remind Turkey of the cost of entering the Western camp over the Syria gridlock.[31] According to this position, Turkey also makes rational calculations to maximize its manoeuvre space in this intricate setting. The same camp asserts that by providing indispensable sanctuary for the Sunni rebels fighting Assad and by training and providing them with arms, Turkey makes its intentions about sponsoring the Sunni cause quite clear.[32] The same sources claim that Turkey either ignores the jihadists trespassing on its soil from Syria or uses them to counter Kurdish insurgents stirred up by the Iranian cells.[33] Those who advance this argument also assert that to gain an upper hand over Iran,

Ankara has favored closer contacts among Sunni Arabs and Kurds in northern Iraq. Turkey's trade volume with northern Iraq has climbed to $8 billion per year compared to only $2 billion with the southern portion of the country, and Ankara is seeking lucrative oil deals with Iraqi Kurds.[34]

According to experts, Ankara's close relations with the Sunni elements galvanizes not only the Assad or former Nouri Al-Maliki regimes but also Hezbollah in Lebanon and the Iranian regime in Tehran to gang up on Turkey.[35] The same host of experts also argues that Iran's retaliation is likely to come in the form of an intervention in Turkey's ethnic fault lines. The other supporters of the proxy war arguments juxtapose Iran as the patron of the Shiite regimes and Saudi Arabia as the custodian of the Sunni brand of Islam. These pundits claim that each power is contending for the other's sphere of influence through the Syrian battlefield. However, they also seem to have unambiguously placed Turkey in the Sunni camp with Saudi Arabia.[36] Furthermore, this group of experts claim that from Washington's perspective, Turkey is also in the same camp as the Muslim Brotherhood. Yet one big difference remains between Turkey and the others: that is, while neither Saudi Arabia nor the Muslim Brotherhood is vested in the democratization of the region, Turkey still cares about the progress in the region toward a more democratic governance structured with the rule of law and fundamental freedoms. While Turkey continues to engage with Sunni-fundamentalist organizations on the bases of ethics, morals, values and fundamental freedoms, its traditional allies, be it in the West of the Gulf, are growing more concerned about Turkey's increasing closeness to these entities. The same group of countries suspect that this type of engagement would cause a new unstable environment in the region.

Iran's Nuclear Programme

Turkey has been one of the most ardent supporters of Iran's nuclear programme for peaceful use. Despite the West's alacrity to ban Iran's research into peaceful nuclear energy once and for all, Turkey, under Prime Minister Erdoğan's personal discretion, has worked tirelessly to alter the Western view on the issue. Turkey's improving relations a priori the Arab uprisings and its dramatically enlarged commercial activity with Iran have been especially alarming to the West, which has sought to diplomatically isolate the Islamic Republic because of its support for terrorism and suspicions over its nuclear programme. Turkey, meanwhile, has sought to use its new relations with Iran to position itself as a bridge between Europe and the pariah state. In January 2011, the five permanent members of the UN Security Council plus Germany, also known as 'P5 + 1', met with the Iranian delegation in Istanbul to discuss Iran's nuclear programme upon Turkey's invitation.

The Istanbul talks were intended to build confidence between the parties and to achieve an agreement that Iran would trade some of its low-enriched uranium for nuclear fuel for Tehran's Research Reactor. Turkey and Brazil were the chief proponents of this plan. The deal failed when the USA and the other parties involved rejected the amount Tehran agreed to transfer to Turkey. The West contended that the amount the Iranian government agreed to release still left sufficient enriched uranium to put together a nuclear weapon. Turkey subsequently protested the West's decision to use its veto at the UN Security Council meeting in June 2010 on the sanctions proposed for Iran. A few more conventions followed suit—the last in line taking place again in Istanbul on 18 March 2013, to little avail.

Fast-forwarding to today, Rouhani's election and the promising nuclear talks with the West seem to have opened a new chapter on Iran's nuclear adventure. Even though the partisan politics in the USA over the normalization of relations with the Islamic Republic, as well as Israel's global campaign to stop a nuclear Iran, can turn the clock back on progress, Iran's nuclear future will not be the same as anticipated before. Despite its own concerns of Iran waging a proxy war as nuclear power, Turkey also finds itself at an opportune crossroads in the aftermath of President Erdoğan's visit to use its diplomatic ties to encourage Iran for further transparency and cooperation at every level. Turkey is also mindful that the overall clauses of the JCPOA assuage its own concerns regarding Iran's access to nuclear weapons. Furthermore, the lifting of sanctions will provide a welcome boost to Turkish trade, which has sustained a serious blow from the decades of sanctions imposed on Iran. Last, Turkey is prepared to contribute to the process as needed in order to help reach a common understanding around a set of constructive measures.

Conclusion

From the recent tensions in the relationship between the two countries, the path ahead of Turkish–Iranian affairs promises to be thorny, unless Iran chooses to focus not on diverging self-interests but on a cooperative policy with Turkey to promote peace and stability in the region. The two dramatically different paths of political development that each country has embarked upon in its post-imperial era resulted in an extroverted, globally/regionally engaged Turkey that is navigating towards a consolidated democracy and an isolated and authoritarian Iran. Whereas Turkey has struggled and aspired to become more engaged with the global actors and exert its influence through the means of regional engagement, Iran utilized its introversion and isolation to entrench its hegemony in its neighbourhood. This divergence stemming from similar—and to a certain extent—converging historical character-istics has eventually led to the two different modes of engagement with the region, which have swung Turkey and Iran to the opposite ends of the spectrum once again. Humanitarian diplomacy will continue to be the steering tenet of Turkish foreign policy for years to come. Turkey's committed engagement to the conflict-affected states in the neighbourhood will prioritize state building, unconditional humanitarian aid and development assistance. Furthermore, Turkey is expected to make a sizeable leap with respect to the 'peace process' with its own Kurdish minority in the aftermath of the 7 June 2015 elections. In other words, the pursuit of humanitarian diplomacy will keep consolidating Turkey's soft power in the region for the foreseeable future. In that regard, Turkey's increased influence in the region may continue to be interpreted as a threat for Iran's hegemonic aspirations.

Yet, with Rouhani's election and the prospect of opening up to the West, Iran is also facing a decisive moment in its history. Domestically, the elimination of the sanctions and Rouhani's embrace of a more reform-oriented governance may help bring the liberalization that all walks of Iranian life have longed for. Political ramifications of this may naturally enable Iranian foreign policy to seek less interest driven, yet more humanitarian outcomes in the region. At this juncture, the foreign policy decisions Tehran may take might change the status quo of the Islamic Republic's engagement with the region and other influential actors such as Turkey and Saudi Arabia. If the Iranian regime chooses to follow a more cooperative foreign and regional policy, there is an ample opportunity for Turkey and Iran to merge their capacities and work towards the joint welfare of their neighbourhood. However, if Tehran opts for nation building and sectarian policies, the regime will risk deterioration of its constructive relations with steadfast patrons and partners like Turkey that vouch relentlessly for Iran's peaceful existence in the international community and the elimination of sanctions. As the calamity in Syria forewarns us, and the progressive developments from Turkey attest, the future dynamics in the region will favour those that have resolved their domestic strife and engaged their region through ethical, moral and constructive values.

Disclosure statement

No potential conflict of interest was reported by the authors.

Notes

[1] The US Department of State, 'Parameters for a Joint Comprehensive Plan of Action Regarding the Islamic Republic of Iran's Nuclear Program', 2 April 2015, <http://www.state. gov/r/pa/prs/ps/2015/04/240170.htm> (accessed 15 May 2015).
[2] A. Davutoğlu, 'Zero problems in a new era', *Foreign Policy*, 21 March 2013, <http:// foreignpolicy.com/2013/03/21/zero-problems-in-a-new-era/> (accessed 15 May 2015).
[3] Ibid.
[4] Ibid.
[5] K. Kirişçi, 'The transformation of Turkish foreign policy: the rise of the trading state', *New Perspectives on Turkey*, 40, 2009, pp. 29–57.
[6] Ibid.
[7] Ibid.
[8] R. Bayer and E. F. Keyman, 'Turkey: an emerging hub of globalization and internationalist humanitarian actor?', *Globalizations*, 9(1), 2012, pp. 73–90.
[9] Ibid.
[10] E. F. Keyman, *Turkey and the Arab Spring*, The Bertelsmann Foundation, Gütersloh, 2012.
[11] K. Derviş, 'The economic imperatives of the Arab Spring', 2011 Year End Series, Project Syndicate, 2011, <www.project-syndicate.org> (accessed 9 March 2012).
[12] Ibid.
[13] B. Aras, 'Turkey and Iran: facing the challenge of the Arab Spring', *GMF on Turkey Series*, 19 February 2013, <http://www.gmfus.org/publications/turkey-and-iran-facing-challenge-arab-spring> (accessed 15 May 2015).
[14] B. Oran (ed.), *Türk Dış Politikası: Kurtuluş Savaşından Bugüne Olgular, Belgeler, Yorumlar* [*Turkish Foreign Policy: From the War of Independence to Today; Concepts, Documents, Comments*], Vol. 3, İletişim Yayıncılık, Istanbul, 2013, p. 453.

[15] M. Şahin, 'Iran: "realistic" foreign policy of a "theocratic and idealistic" state', *USAK Yearbook*, USAK, Ankara, 2012, pp. 279–281.

[16] Aras, op. cit.

[17] Ibid.

[18] 'İran Arap Baharına Nasıl Bakıyor?', *SETA*, <http://www.setav.org/tr/%C4%B0ran-arap-baharina-nasil-bakiyor/haber/1294> (accessed 15 May 2015).

[19] K. Dalacoura, 'The Arab uprisings two years on: ideology, sectarianism and the changing balance of power in the Middle East', *Insight Turkey*, 15(1), 2013, pp. 75–89.

[20] Aras, op. cit., p. 3.

[21] Şahin, op. cit., p. 279.

[22] Ibid., p. 281.

[23] Aras, op. cit., p. 3.

[24] Oran, op. cit., p. 453.

[25] Ibid.

[26] M. Morell, 'Iran's grand strategy is to become a regional powerhouse', *The Washington Post*, 3 April 2015, <http://www.washingtonpost.com/opinions/irans-grand-strategy/2015/04/03/415ec8a8-d8a3-11e4-ba28-f2a685dc7f89_story.html> (accessed 15 May 2015).

[27] Ibid.

[28] Ibid.

[29] Ibid.

[30] B. Özkan, 'America, Turkey and Saudi Arabia are pouring fuel on the fire in Syria', *The Huffington Post*, 15 May 2015, <http://www.huffingtonpost.com/behlal-azkan/america-turkey-saudi-arabia-syria_b_7278586.html> (accessed 15 May 2015). Also, see Aaron Stein, 'Turkey's Yemen dilemma', *Foreign Affairs*, 7 April 2015, <https://www.foreignaffairs.com/articles/turkey/2015-04-07/turkeys-yemen-dilemma > (accessed 15 May 2015).

[31] S. Çağaptay, 'Turkey's foray into the Fertile Crescent', *The International Herald Tribune*, 28 February 2013, p. 6. Also, see H. M. Karaveli, 'The unhelpful ally', *The International Herald Tribune*, 28 February 2013, p. 6.

[32] Karaveli, op. cit., p. 6.

[33] Ibid.

[34] Çağaptay, op. cit., p. 6.

[35] S. Cengiz, 'Turkey should brace itself against expected proxy wars in 2013', *Today's Zaman*, 13 January 2013, <http://www.todayszaman.com/news-303853-turkey-should-brace-itself-against-expected-proxy-wars-in-2013.html> (accessed 18 March 2013).

[36] Ö. Taşpınar, 'Turkey and Saudi Arabia: strange bedfellows in Syria', *Today's Zaman*, 3 December 2012, <http://www.todayszaman.com/columnist-299995-turkey-and-saudi-arabia-strange-bedfellows-in-syria.html> (accessed 13 January 2013).

E. Fuat Keyman is Director of the Istanbul Policy Center and Professor of International Relations at Sabanci University in Istanbul. Keyman is a leading Turkish political scientist and expert on democratization, globalization, international relations, Turkey–EU relations, Turkish foreign policy and civil society development. He is a member of the Science Academy. He has worked as a member on the Council of Wise People as part of the Peace Process to the Kurdish issue. He also serves on advisory and editorial boards for a number of respected international and national organizations, as well as academic journals.

Onur Sazak is Research and Academic Affairs Manager at Istanbul Policy Center (IPC). Sazak joined IPC in 2010 as Research and Academic Affairs Coordinator. Prior to his tenure at IPC, he worked as Research Associate at Hudson Institute in Washington, DC. At Hudson, he was part of the Center for Eurasian Policy, where he focused on a wide array of research, from energy security to the trends of political Islam in Central Asia and Europe. Sazak received his BA in International Relations and MA in International Economic Relations from American University in Washington, DC. He is currently pursuing a PhD in Political Science at Sabanci University.

Turkish Foreign Policy towards the Arab Spring: Between Western Orientation and Regional Disorder

Emirhan Yorulmazlar and Ebru Turhan

Turkey's foreign policy approach towards the Middle East and North Africa (MENA) region has been predicated on an integrationist vision through cooperation and dialogue over the past decade. The Arab Spring significantly challenged Turkey's role as a strategic interconnector and set the stage for broader debates on foreign policy orientation. This paper suggests that any fair assessment of Ankara's performance in the MENA must take into account the significant constraints imposed on Turkish foreign policy objectives by regional power rivalries and growing Western detachment from the region. The paper sheds light on the impact of global and regional powers' responses to the Arab Spring for Middle Eastern order and outlines a possible trajectory for the transformation of Turkish foreign policy to ensure effective Turkish activism in the post-Arab Spring environment.

Introduction

Over the past decade, Turkey has redefined its relations with the countries of the Middle East and North Africa (MENA). A multifaceted and holistic conceptual framework, which was predicated on an integrationist vision through cooperation and dialogue, has replaced Ankara's predominantly security-driven and discreet engagement in the MENA region. This new approach has expanded Turkey's scope of influence in the region and increased its allure and importance in the eyes of Western allies, as the Turkish model appeared to have successfully reconciled Islam with democratic and economic reform. Turkey has served as a strategic interconnector between regional interlocutors, as well as between the West and the Middle East.

The popular uprisings that have come to be known as the Arab Spring have significantly challenged Turkey's role as a strategic interconnector and set the stage for broader debates on foreign policy orientation. While Ankara's response over time has diverged from its Western allies,[1] it has also put Turkey's relations with its immediate neighbourhood to a challenging test. On that note, Turkish foreign policy towards the MENA region has underscored the need for a redefinition of Turkey's broader role and orientation.

This paper suggests that any fair assessment of Ankara's performance in the MENA region must take into account the significant constraints imposed on Turkish foreign policy objectives and instruments by regional power rivalries and security dilemmas against growing Western detachment from the region. In this context, the main aim of this paper is to examine the implications of global and regional powers' responses to the Arab Spring for Middle Eastern order and outline a possible trajectory for the transformation of Turkish foreign policy in order to ensure a sustainable and effective role for Turkey to promote its objective of ensuring regional stability and security. The paper first scrutinizes the conceptual and structural bases of major shifts in Turkish foreign policy in the pre-Arab Spring period. It then outlines the challenges for Western–Turkish cooperation in the MENA region by providing a critical assessment of the key components and determinants of Western response to the Arab Spring and the resultant geopolitical landscape. The paper subsequently reveals the complexity of the regional setting and formulates a set of policy recommendations for effective Turkish activism in the post-Arab Spring environment.

Turkish Foreign Policy before the Arab Spring

Following the 'longest decade'[2] in the post-Cold War period, which was compounded by regional and ethnic conflicts, the turn of the millennium ushered in a new era of constructive engagement in Turkish foreign policy. This transition was nowhere more visible than in Turkey's relations with the Middle Eastern countries.[3] Thus, Turkey moved from its traditionally detached course to seek a new role as a stakeholder in regional affairs. Turkish activism was largely built upon an ideational turn, which came to define Turkey as a historical and cultural part—and even the natural leader— of the region.[4]

The Justice and Development Party (JDP), a successor of Turkey's conservative right and traditional Islamic parties, initially espoused a double course in foreign policy in what Robbins called co-optation of 'two traditions'.[5] As Western orientation kept its central place in Turkish foreign policy with the accentuated Europeanization process, a regional policy was simultaneously being crafted to reconstruct Turkish clout in the neighbourhood. The European Union (EU) accession process enabled the JDP to stabilize its political position and, in a way, was instrumentalized as a tool of domestic transformation.[6] The ensuing reforms paved the way not only for domestic consolidation but also for the JDP government to incrementally build a power base particularly in the Middle East.

The JDP's first electoral term was thus marked by attempts at establishing Turkey's regional role hand in hand with the EU accession process. The JDP foreign policy was peculiar in its attempt to balance and consolidate Western orientation with an active regional policy, which owed largely to a strong belief in the multicultural character of Turkey. A number of conjunctural developments were undoubtedly conducive in paving the way for this regional engagement, dubbed as 'the zero-problems policy (ZPP)'.[7] First, the unilateralism of the USA and the ensuing instability in the Middle East prepared ample ground to recast Turkey as an effective regional actor with increasing soft power.[8] The Turkish refusal to participate and support the American-led coalition forces' invasion of Iraq also highlighted Ankara's independent and, in a way, legitimate role free of 'Western tutelage'. Second, Ankara has reached out to almost all political groups and conflicting actors, turning itself into an honest broker. Intensification of relations with the Arab states and Iran, on top of traditional ties with pro-Western regimes, put Turkey in an advantageous position. This inclusive approach also laid the groundwork for later mediation efforts. Third, at a time when Paris, Berlin and other EU capitals stood against the American hegemonic pretensions, the EU accession process enabled Ankara to also stand for dialogue, cooperation, good governance and civilian rule in the neighbourhood. This in turn empowered the 'Turkish model', which symbolized an attempt to implement Western values in a Muslim-majority country. Last but not least, the possibility of a regional redesign in the name of 'the Greater Middle East' put PKK (Kurdistan Workers' Party) terrorism on the back burner and pointed to the need for a more comprehensive and integrated approach to regional security and stability, which justified Turkish engagement with other regional actors.

Gaining the upper hand in domestic politics after 2007, the JDP government moved on to actively pursue the goal of assuming a leading regional and, ideally, global role. Yet while regional attempts expanded, the Europeanization process reached a stall. This, in turn, set the stage for a debate on Turkey's 'shift of axis', that is, the erosion of Turkey's predominantly Western orientation.[9] While Turkish policymakers categorically denied arguments to that effect, Turkish foreign policy indisputably opted for an autonomous and self-perpetuating course, which occasionally diverged or converged with Western partners.

This quest for autonomy, which has traditionally been one of the defining principles of Turkish foreign policy, did not necessarily point to realignment. Growing divergences also triggered an ideational policy change, which no longer approached relations with the West from an identity and commitment point of view in the traditional sense.[10] As such, Turkish foreign policy activism sought convergence with Western partners, this time based primarily on common interests. This strategy, however, rather than supporting harmonization with the EU, contradictorily led to increasing cooperation and consultation with the USA in the JDP's second term.[11] This pragmatic approach, in turn, rendered divergent Turkish moves, such as confrontation with Israel and rapprochement with Iran and Syria, more palpable within the larger framework of the Western alliance.

The combination of the JDP's growing domestic and foreign policy autonomy paved the way for more concrete Turkish moves towards an integrated Middle Eastern order. To that end, Ankara engaged all possible interlocutors to deepen economic and political relations with Middle Eastern countries and appeared willing to overcome traditional security concerns. This approach benefitted from the relative authoritarian stability in the region, particularly following the final suppression of the latest wave of popular demands in Syria, Egypt, Saudi Arabia and Iran in 2005. Turkish activism also included mediation efforts for conflict resolution such as Israel–Syria indirect talks, proximity talks among Iraqi ethnic groups and Iranian nuclear talks. Moreover, Turkey came to accept the transnational nature of the Kurdish question and engaged the Kurdistan Regional Government (KRG) in Iraq to counter the cross-border attacks while initiating a behind-the-scenes domestic reconciliation process with the Kurds. Overall, these attempts were designed to elevate the Turkish status to a regional leadership role.

With the advent of the Arab Spring, however, Turkish foreign policy's modus operandi has completely changed. In the beginning, an optimistic interpretation of the popular revolts prevailed among Turkish policymakers. Thus, a more conducive regional order was thought to be in the making, seen as an eventual corollary of doing away with the Cold War mentality.[12] A chain of like-minded governments assumed power from Libya to Egypt and Tunisia to vindicate Turkey's soft power of emulation. In Ankara the thinking was that this would pave the way to overcome the perennial question of the 'incompatibility' of Islam and democracy. A compatible mode in turn would strengthen Turkey's case for EU membership as Turkey was leading the normative shift in favour of 'universal' values in the Islamic world. The USA's reading of events initially overlapped with the Turkish interpretation, which further emboldened Turkish policymakers to welcome the regional transformation. Yet it was not long before this coexistential understanding of the West–Islam relationship faced realpolitik considerations and crumbled before Western inaction and regional power rivalries.

EU, USA and the Lost Opportunity of the Arab Spring

Until the onset of the Arab Spring, the EU's experience with the MENA region in the post-Cold War era was predominantly founded on initiatives such as the Euro-Mediterranean Partnership (EMP) and European Neighbourhood Policy (ENP). These arrangements largely addressed the economic relations between the EU and its wider neighbourhood without explicitly linking cooperation to democratic conditionality. In 2008, the EU launched the Union for the Mediterranean (UfM) to apply a more holistic approach to the Euro-Mediterranean dialogue by addressing manifold concerns such as democracy, energy, economy, environment, migration and health. Yet the UfM failed to deliver upon its initial objectives due to three core reasons. First, the intergovernmentalist institutional architecture of the UfM excluded societal actors from policymaking processes. This obstructed the establishment of inclusive processes of dialogue for the promotion of democracy and inclusive economic growth in the MENA region.[13] Second, French preferences predominantly shaped the UfM agenda, thereby weakening the multilateral framework of the cooperation.[14] Third, the EU's own north–south split across the Mediterranean brought about difficulties pertaining to the creation of common policies vis-à-vis the region. On that note, in the pre-Arab Spring era, the role of the EU as an agent of democracy promotion in its wider neighbourhood remained considerably constrained by supply-driven mechanisms and instruments.

Following the outbreak of the Arab uprisings, the EU first sought to deploy demand-driven instruments in the MENA by centring its initiatives around the empowerment of domestic societal actors and becoming a more engaged agent of democracy promotion. In particular, it launched three important programmes to promote the involvement of domestic constituencies in agenda-setting and policymaking: the SPRING Program (Support for Partnership, Reform and Inclusive Growth); the Neighborhood Civil Society Facility; and the European Endowment for Democracy (EED).[15] Furthermore, the EU founded one of the key pillars of its dialogue with the MENA on positive conditionality by introducing the 'more-for-more' approach, which linked the Union's support for more money, mobility and market access in the region—known as the '3 Ms'—to the progress in undertaking reforms.

This demand-driven foreign policy approach was soon exposed to supply-driven constraints as a result of security objectives of the EU and its member states, ranging from the control of irregular migration to counterterrorism to the supply of energy security. The management of migration flows from the MENA following the outbreak of the uprisings has been of great concern to the EU, particularly to the Mediterranean member states. The number of refugees and asylum seekers arriving in Italy rose from 43,000 in 2013 to 160,000 in 2014, with the extraordinary pace of 14,700 arrivals per month.[16] As a result of this migration influx, the EU's post-Arab Spring policy approach demonstrated a strong security focus on migration. This has been reflected in the EU's intensification of its border controls and surveillance policies and its adoption of various programmes like Mobility Partnerships and the Dialogues for Migration, Mobility and Security with the Southern Mediterranean. These programmes culminated in an asymmetrical relationship between the two parties, with MENA countries having been obliged to toughen their border controls and cooperate with Frontex as an exchange for vaguely defined legal immigration prospects to the EU.[17] The EU has launched similar initiatives and programmes to secure the supply of energy and decrease its dependency on Russian gas. As part of its 'more-for-more' approach, it has initiated cooperation activities such as the Euro-Arab Mashreq Gas Market Project and the Euro-Mediterranean Energy Market Integration Project (MED-EMIP). However, as a result of the asymmetry in bilateral energy trade relations between the EU and these countries, the EU's positive conditionality strategy has been ineffective in bringing about the desired outcomes and the promotion of democracy in energy-exporting countries like Libya and Algeria.[18]

With the onset of the Arab Spring, the security objectives and economic interests of the EU reinforced the realpolitik rationale for foreign policymaking towards the MENA, culminating in inadequate European action on democracy concerns in the region. Weak European commitment to the promotion of liberal democratic values has been reinforced by the fragmentation of EU member states as a result of diverging interests and threat perceptions, and the negative consequences of the Eurozone crisis for the European economies. The crisis has put significant constraints on the time, money and attention devoted to foreign policymaking within EU circles.[19] The EU budget's share for external action shrank from 6.4 per cent in 2012 to 4.8 per cent in 2013.[20]

The intergovernmental and interest-driven institutional architecture of EU-led initiatives in the MENA region, accompanied by the EU's own internal crises, obstructed its effective cooperation with traditional powers such as the USA and other influential actors in the region including Turkey and the countries of the Gulf

Cooperation Council (GCC). The EU's overlooking of joint action opportunities with major external actors was an important shortcoming of the 2011 review of the ENP. As Nathalie Tocci observes, 'the EU, in its ENP review, continues to think it acts in a vacuum, failing to seize on the synergies and contrast the eventual counter of the multiple sets of actors involved in the region'.[21] Indeed, although the European Commission's 2014 Progress Report on Turkey and its 2014/15 Enlargement Strategy reaffirmed that Turkey is a key strategic partner for the Union, joint EU–Turkey cooperation in the region largely lacked institutional and strategic commitment through regular dialogue between the Turkish Cooperation and Coordination Agency (TIKA) and the Commission's Directorate-General for International Cooperation and Development (DG DEVCO), and other EU initiatives like the EED.

Alongside the adoption of inward-looking and supply-driven policy approaches by the EU towards the MENA, Turkey's painfully slow accession talks with the EU have been particularly challenging for Turkish–European cooperation in post-Arab Spring countries. Economic relations between Turkey and the EU have gradually improved, especially thanks to the multiplier effect of the customs union agreement between both parties. However, the stall in Turkey's political integration into the EU, reinforced by the successive vetoes of the Council of the EU and some member states on talks over major chapters of the acquis, has not only led to the rise of Euroscepticism amongst the Turkish public but has also appeared to have lessened the incentives for Turkey to align its foreign policy with the EU. Between 2007 and 2014, Ankara's alignment with EU declarations and Council decisions pertaining to the Common Foreign and Security Policy (CFSP) decreased from 98 per cent to a remarkable 29 per cent.[22]

The coordination of Turkish–Western responses to the Arab Spring was further challenged by the inconsistencies and oscillation in US foreign policy vis-à-vis the uprisings. The Arab Spring increased the already existing dilemma between strategic interests and values in US foreign policy as it required both the maintenance of stability and the promotion of democracy through the overthrow of the authoritarian regimes in the MENA region. As Juan Cole states, 'The Arab Spring put him [Obama] in a very difficult position. [. . .] As a world power, you don't want to lose your allies. As a democratic world power, you don't want to be opposed to democratizing.'[23] In fact, in the post-September 11 era, the USA prioritized cooperation with existing authoritarian regimes over democracy promotion in the MENA. Nader Hashemi has accurately noted that '[g]reater democracy does not always translate into greater support for US geo-strategic interests in the region'.[24] The uprisings in the Arab world initially culminated in increased rhetorical support by the Obama administration for the promotion of human rights, rule of law and transition to democracy in the region.[25] However, this understanding was soon replaced by a more inward-looking and interest-driven approach, particularly following the 2012 US consulate attack in Benghazi and the use of chemical weapons in Syria against civilians. Given its country-specific security and economic interests, the Obama administration attempted to deal with each uprising on a case-by-case and ad hoc basis, which led to incoherence within and between the US response in each country.[26] Possible US activism was further undermined by growing domestic political polarization and national reluctance for new foreign policy adventures.

In a nutshell, since the onset of the Arab Spring, Western reaction to changing political, economic and social landscapes has been predominantly shaped by security and economic interests, domestic constraints and intergovernmental institutional mechanisms. The domestication of Western policies vis-à-vis the MENA imposed significant constraints on the role of the West as an agent of democracy promotion, as well as Western–Turkish cooperation in the region. Western–Turkish joint efforts have been further obstructed by the weakening of Turkey's political dialogue with the EU, which led to insufficient communication between the two parties regarding their preferences and interests pertaining to the region. Increasing regional rivalries accompanied by continuous and multidimensional power struggles in the post-Arab Spring geopolitical landscape have further complicated Western–Turkish joint actions and imposed significant constraints on Turkish foreign policy options.

The Post-Arab Spring Geopolitical Panorama

The Arab Spring undermined the main pillars of the regional order by steering different power struggles and rivalries, as well as intra- and interstate sectarian fragmentation, in the MENA region and by fostering the ability of extremist non-state actors to gain ground in unstable territories with significant power vacuums. The resultant turbulence required a constant recalculation of foreign policy preferences by the new governments and the existing authoritarian regimes of the region, and the regional chaos has already had deep global consequences.

At first, the uprisings triggered optimism, but after a while a security dilemma scenario emerged among the Iranian political elite. Initially, Iran welcomed the uprisings as a movement that would transform the Arab world in accordance with the principles and ideologies embraced by the Islamic Republic.[27] It misperceived the revolts, which were rather indispensable consequences of political and socio-economic disparities in the region, as a de facto Islamic awakening. Accordingly, at the start of the uprisings, the Iranian political elite tolerated the unconditional support of the local media for revolts against authoritarian regimes[28] and welcomed the overthrow of Mubarak in Egypt. However, the Arab Spring did not foster the attractiveness of the Iranian model among the Arab world. It rather altered the key parameters of regional politics—culminating in the intensification of sectarian polarization and downplaying the struggle against Israel on the one hand, and increasing proxy battles between Shia Iran and the members of the Sunni-ruled GCC on the other.

The escalation of the sectarian divide in the post-Arab Spring political landscape was accompanied by fears of revolts spreading to Iran. The parallels between the 2011 Arab Spring and the 2009 Iranian Green Movement increased Tehran's risk and threat perception and its willingness to defend the regional status quo. On that note, Iran responded to the uprisings via 'continuous recalculation of policies' to preserve its core interests.[29] Whereas Tehran backed the fall of Mubarak in Egypt, it saw strategic benefits in supporting the preservation of the Assad regime in Syria. Iranian leadership has explicitly opposed the GCC's military intervention in Bahrain and to a lesser extent in Yemen, yet avoided direct confrontation with Saudi Arabia. Iran's rather inarticulate foreign policy approach vis-à-vis the Arab Spring imposed significant constraints on its relations with key regional actors such as Turkey and the members of the GCC, whose struggle against Iran has been further reinforced by suspicions over shifting balances of power in the Middle East following the interim nuclear deal between Iran and the USA.[30]

Following the onset of the Arab Spring, the Saudi–Iranian rivalry has propagated military activism in the region. The Saudi Arabian regime supported both NATO (North Atlantic Treaty Organization) military intervention against the Gaddafi regime in Libya and the revolutionary fractions in Syria, and militarily intervened in the Bahrain revolts. In doing so, Riyadh sought to preserve the royal sheikhdom system of governance and hamper the expansion of Iranian influence in the region. US reluctance to fully engage its diplomatic and military capabilities in the post-Arab Spring geopolitical landscape compelled regional powers to fill in the leadership gap. Therefore, the Iranian regime attempted to preserve—even reinforce—its regional power status with the empowerment of the Shia sphere of the region throughout the uprisings. Yet the recent activism of Saudi Arabia in Syria and Yemen supported by other Arab regimes and Turkey is testament to regional backlash against Iranian projections in the region.

The increased confrontation between Russia and the West has further complicated the rapidly evolving post-Arab Spring geopolitical landscape. Contrary to the Western practice, Russian leadership has shown great reluctance to support the uprisings and the fall of the authoritarian regimes due to three major considerations. First, Moscow saw parallels between the Arab revolts and the domestic electoral tension that occurred in Russia during the 2011 parliamentary and 2012 presidential elections.[31] Second, the political and economic turmoil in the transition countries led to significant losses in the Russian defence industry as a result of the termination of several defence contracts.[32] Third, Russian leadership has traditionally defended the principle of non-interference in sovereign states' internal affairs, and the determination of a regime's destiny by domestic dynamics rather than military interventions of external actors.[33] Having chosen not to veto the 2011 United Nations (UN) Security Council resolution on Libya, Moscow toughened its stance towards the West and intensified its attempts to position itself in the region as an alternative to the EU and USA, following the expansion of the UN mandate from humanitarian goals to military intervention. Russia's endeavours to enhance its regional position vis-à-vis the West and its sphere of interests have found life in its firm position against regime change in Syria and its confrontational stance towards the Ukraine crisis in 2014, which the Russian leadership perceived as 'an EU-assisted *coup d'état* happening on its doorstep'.[34]

Contrary to the attempts of many regional powers to play a more active role in the formation of the post-Arab Spring order, the Israeli government preferred to keep a rather low profile throughout the uprisings given both its external constraints and the implications of shifting regional dynamics for its dialogue with neighbouring actors. As far as external constraints are concerned, given public opinion's hostile stance against Israel in transition countries and the rising influence of popular demands in domestic preference formation, the Israeli leadership took a wait-and-see approach to monitor the attention paid by the new governments to public attitudes.[35] Israel's increasing political isolation—partly due to waning US influence in the Middle East, as well as the Obama administration's abortive efforts to find a diplomatic solution to the Israeli–Palestinian conflict—reinforced Israeli reluctance to take an overly active and risk-prone role in shaping the regional order. That being said, Israel's concerns about 'Islamist extremism' and Iran's quest for regional hegemony have been largely shared by other Middle Eastern countries like Saudi Arabia, Egypt and Jordan. Such shared security concerns and preferences have fostered the preservation of Israel's ad hoc bilateral cooperation with the axis of pro-Western states in the region.[36]

Post-Arab Spring interstate rivalries over regional hegemony, accompanied by greater sectarian fragmentation and political turmoil in transition countries, provided the non-state actors with many opportunities to fill the power vacuum in the MENA region. While the growing clout of Hezbollah, the KRG and various militia groups carries the potential to undo the political map of the region, the sudden and unexpected territorial expansion of the Islamic State (ISIS) in particular has already had a profound effect on both regional and global security. Alongside the implications for broader regional upheaval, Western concerns over radicalization and the execution of terrorist attacks by European and North American foreign fighters point to the global dimension of the ISIS phenomenon.[37]

Turkey's New Geopolitics

The devolution of the Arab Spring into a traumatic experience for regional and global order overturned Turkish designs for a leading role in the MENA region. Thereafter, Ankara backpedalled on its earlier claim as an 'order-instituting [regional] power' and was unable to lead efforts to halt regional security competition. Today, Turkey faces a chaotic regional order in the Middle East against its own weakening Western links.

The Middle East has entered another cycle of turbulence. The global and regional actors largely failed to quell regional instability, and instead exacerbated it. Yet the ongoing multidimensional conflict will only subside in the case of a coordinated effort by global and regional powers towards a stable and sustainable settlement, which is currently predicated on what Crooke called 'an equilibrium of antagonisms'.[38] Unable to remake the Middle East in its mirror image, Turkey has been caught in the middle of these antagonisms, which eventually unleashed the sectarian, extremist and ethnonationalist threats all undermining the fundamentals of regional order.

Against this backdrop, Turkey's options are thought to have been squeezed between a fight for supremacy or to revert to traditional detachment.[39] However, this is a miscalculation that builds either on an imperial or strictly nationalist vision. Turkey cannot depend on a 'win or lose' approach and needs to continue constructing channels of dialogue with Western and regional interlocutors. To this end, a reassessment of the reasons for the failure of the regional transitions and

Turkey's available assets to overcome these is a prerequisite for a sustainable regional role.

The failure of the regional attempt towards a popular order beyond determinant internal dynamics stemmed basically from three external factors. First, the lack of a powerful anchor willing to take the risk to lead the revolts to a normative regional order; second, the clash of geopolitical rivalries, as predominant actors have been unable to cooperate on a common denominator for the region's future; third, regional and global insecurities about the unknown, that is, an alternative order that could have undone prevailing vested interests. As a result, Turkish foreign policy needs to take into account these reasons for failure in its quest to steer the region out of the ongoing turbulence.

Turkey's ability to steer the region into its preferred course on its own is limited and hence, depends on building coalitions. Therefore, Turkey is well advised to seek closer cooperation and consultation with its Western partners. There is much room for joint action particularly on security, counterterrorism, refugees and economic development of the region. Turkey's quest for multilateral action on countering the crises also entails Western support especially in the UN Security Council, NATO and the EU. Moreover, the Turkish case for democratization in the region largely overlaps with the ultimate Western call for regional liberalization. However, given Western reluctance for further involvement, Turkey would have to work on a selective agenda with Western partners and, therefore, would need to keep a closer eye on regional balance of power.

To ensure regional security and stability, Turkey needs to help defuse geopolitical rivalries and possibly assume a mediator role to seek a middle ground.[40] The Iran–Saudi rivalry is not only weakening the pillars of regional order but also consumes these two countries' capabilities and carries the risk of undermining their domestic balances. To avert a possible doomsday scenario, that is, unravelling of the political borders and further fragmentation, Turkey is among the few countries that could bridge the widening gap between Tehran and Riyadh, which has been aggravated by the prospect of an Iranian nuclear deal. A coordinated effort on hotspots such as Syria and Yemen might facilitate the long-awaited political transitions, which would ameliorate the burgeoning sectarian and extremist threats. Geostrategic considerations aside, what Iran wants for Yemen and Saudi Arabia calls for Syria are indeed the recipes for peaceful transition in both countries, that is, ending foreign intervention, regional reconciliation and letting people decide their own political futures, which have been propagated by Turkey since the beginning of the crises.

Overcoming the insecurities about an alternative order is a greater challenge, which is further complicated by the complex and multifaceted relations between regional and global actors. The American war fatigue and European economic slowdown not only minimized Western involvement but also came to threaten the basics of the post-First World War regional order based on nation-states with disputable borders. The still-evolving and unclear 'Obama doctrine'[41] that foresees engaging adversaries and implicitly keeping allies at arm's length has undone the regional balances between pro- and anti-American actors and, even worse, pretends to consider the resultant instability as manageable. The American reluctance to lead regional transformation eventually ended in a re-embrace of 'authoritarian stability', based on a delusional belief in the continuation of the *ancien régimes*.[42]

The regional response to the Arab revolts has generally been reactive, shaped in large part by a willingness to defend the status quo rather than lead the change. Iran and Saudi Arabia as two active powers intervened militarily in their self-assigned spheres of influence to keep protégés in power, namely, regimes in Bahrain, Yemen, Egypt, Syria and, to an extent, Iraq. Both countries saw possible normative change towards popular rule and pluralization as threats to their domestic order and rationalized countermeasures in sectarian and geostrategic terms. Meanwhile, concerns about Western 'encroachments' motivated Russian leadership to stand behind anti-Western forces, which further complicated the transition processes.

Turkey's inability to perpetuate its preferred course of political and economic cooperation was due to first a lack of commitment by regional and Western partners to a common vision; and, second, the securitization of political processes through proxy wars. Unless there appears a spillover from the Middle East in the form of a national security threat, the West would not move to invest in stabilizing the regional order. Therefore, de-securitizing regional confrontation and attempting to lay the groundwork for regional cooperation appears as a more feasible approach to regional policy.

The Middle Eastern crises ultimately call for a new settlement. Long-term political transition would entail a peace treaty not only ending the ongoing civil and proxy wars but also framing the defining elements of the new order, which would be less Western and more local, but would in the end reflect the regional balance of power. It would also have to register the interests of global powers in a 'regional multilateralist' arrangement.[43] Cessation of hostilities is another option, yet it would likely prove ephemeral as it would not address political and, more importantly, sectarian concerns.

Turkey should undertake an active role to ensure regional reconciliation and work on the terms of a peace settlement that would include pro- and anti-Western actors. The Iranian–Saudi rivalry has turned into a systemic risk, and Turkey has the potential to lead the quest for a way out. Internalizing the concerns of non-state actors might be possible within the framework of a larger sectarian reconciliation. For defining the elements of the new order, the Iraqi case set a failed precedent. The federal system, which was designed to represent the different ethnic and sectarian interests, has proven dysfunctional. On the contrary, the centripetal and centrifugal forces clashed, and intercommunal mistrust widened. In the end, not only the Iraqi central authority became paralysed but also moderate forces were crowded out to the detriment of political decision-making.

The Syrian case is even more difficult given a more fragmented and delicate ethno-cultural structure. The idea of keeping the state institutions intact is a lesson learned from Iraq, yet it should not lead to settling down for a semblance of stability under the Assad regime. The plans for a post-Assad Syria should rather work on eliminating the scars of the civil war and introduce possibly a confessional arrangement for a viable political system. A possible reconciliation in Syria and Yemen would in turn pave the way for a wider regional settlement that could be extended to other transitional countries such as Iraq, Libya and Egypt.

Against growing regional instability, Turkey would preferably prioritize domestic concerns, that is, security, economic development and Kurdish reconciliation. Yet all three are organically linked with prevailing trends in the Middle East. Therefore, Turkey needs to work out a new strategy based on three elements.

First, Turkey needs to introduce new instruments for a post-American regional order. While the USA is downsizing its commitments in the Middle East, Ankara has to supplement its reliance on the American security umbrella and enter into additional bilateral and multilateral engagements to overcome burgeoning transnational security threats. Though Turkey as 'a trading state'[44] has certain limitations that would hinder countering the asymmetric power play through proxies, it still has political and economic weight to change the balances in its favour. Therefore, Ankara has to make sure the regional game centres around economic development as opposed to the current wars of attrition. To this end, possible Turkey–EU cooperation would function as a pre-emptive attempt to arrest the growing security and socio-economic problems in the region. On the other hand, a renewed Turkish effort to strengthen political and commercial ties with interlocutors open for dialogue would pave the way for new opportunities.

Second, Turkey should become a stronger voice in the region against extremism and sectarianism. Despite Turkish concerns about the lack of a comprehensive strategy against ISIS and the Assad regime, the public reflections on whether Turkey is unwilling to fight ISIS or prioritizing Assad's downfall have undermined Turkish outreach in the region. As Turkey's president, Recep Tayyip Erdoğan, recently emphasized,[45] Turkey should be a more vocal and active force in the fight against extremism and to that end should engage Western and regional partners. Ankara should also ponder novel ways of curbing the growing power of Shia militias without alienating mainstream Shiite groups.

Success in containment of radical actors would not only open up a new link with moderate actors but also empower the Turkish case for regional stability. Laying the groundwork for Turkish–Saudi–Iranian cooperation in Syria, ideally supported by Western and Arab countries as well, could be a game changer in the region and would be exemplary in curbing sectarianism. If Iran sticks to its geopolitical ambitions, Turkey would seek alternative coalitions to reinstitute regional stability, which was lately epitomized by Turkey–Saudi Arabia–Qatar joint efforts in Syria. Yet in any case, it would be too much to expect a Turkish firefighter role without either Western or regional support.

Third, in an interrelated sense, Turkish activism against extremism would be a boon for the Kurdish reconciliation process, which has undeniably been damaged by mutual incriminations concerning Kobani. Turkey was accused of not doing enough, while the Kurds' appetite for political maximalism fed into the growing mistrust between the parties. One way or the other, a broader dialogue with the Kurds on regional issues would serve Turkey's domestic and regional interests.

The complexities that have been offshoots of regional and global unravelling have come to exhaust the quest for ideal scenarios in the MENA region. Therefore, Turkey should rather work on formulas that would protect its political and economic interests with a long-term view. In fact, the changing dynamics in Turkish politics might point to refocusing on economic priorities after the June 2015 parliamentary elections. On that note, the conclusion of an Iranian deal would open up new venues for economic cooperation, and the possibility of Iran re-emerging as a global energy player might serve to achieve Turkey's designs as an 'energy hub'. The ongoing economic cooperation with Russia, Azerbaijan and Iraq indeed underlines the prospects for a growing Turkish role. Ankara also needs to fall in tune with the GCC countries and possibly develop a more cooperative tone in the Eastern Mediterranean that would prioritize economic ties and develop a common understanding for regional cooperation.

Conclusion

The post-Arab Spring disorder in the Middle East has reinforced the changes in Turkey's foreign policy objectives and tools. The evolving Turkish goal to balance Western orientation with regional ties faces not only the breakdown of regional order but also a downsizing of Western engagement with the Middle East. On that note, Turkey is no longer in a position to play the role of a strategic interconnector, which in turn points to the need to compartmentalize relations with the West and the Middle East.

The paper outlined a possible trajectory to steer the region out of the current geopolitics of turbulence. The absence of ideal solutions against the cross-cutting and conflicting nature of regional and global rivalries has turned the region into a playground of antagonisms. Against this hostile mood, Turkey needs to put its best efforts into changing the region's direction towards compromise and, if possible, cooperation. This commitment might occasionally entail realpolitik to lay the groundwork for possible regional cooperation and inclusion of popular demands through political change. To operate this complex game plan, however, would alternatively entail cooperation, co-optation or even confrontation. In the case of failure, the systemic crisis carries the risk of undermining Turkey's security and domestic political balances.

Disclosure Statement

No potential conflict of interest was reported by the authors.

Notes

[1] See on this, 'Turkey 2012 Progress Report', *European Commission*, SWD (2012) 336, Brussels, 10 October 2012, p. 87, <http://ec.europa.eu/enlargement/pdf/key_documents/2012/package/tr_rapport-_2012_en.pdf> (accessed 7 April 2015); 'Turkey 2013 Progress Report', *European Commission*, SWD (2013) 417, Brussels, 16 October 2013, p. 75, <http://ec.europa.eu/enlargement/pdf/key_documents/2013/-package/tr_rapport_2013.pdf> (accessed 7 April 2015).

[2]   The 1990s were called 'the longest decade' to denote Turkey's national security and foreign policy challenges in the post-Cold War era. See G. Özcan and Ş. Kut (eds), *En Uzun Onyıl: Türkiye'nin Ulusal Güvenlik ve Dış Politika Gündeminde Doksanlı Yıllar*, Boyut Kitapları, Istanbul, 1998.

[3]   S. Larrabee, 'Turkey rediscovers the Middle East', *Foreign Affairs*, 86(4), 2007.

[4]   Ahmet Davutoğlu, *Stratejik Derinlik: Türkiye'nin Uluslararası Konumu* [*Strategic Depth: The International Position of Turkey*], Küre Yayınları, Istanbul, 2001.

[5]   P. Robins, 'Turkish foreign policy since 2002: between a "post-Islamist" government and a Kemalist state', *International Affairs*, 83(2), 2007, pp. 289–304.

[6]   B. Duran, 'JDP and foreign policy as an agent of transformation', in Hakan Yavuz (ed.), *The Emergence of a New Turkey: Democracy and the AK Parti*, University of Utah Press, Salt Lake City, 2006, pp. 281–305.

[7]   A. Davutoğlu, 'Turkey's zero-problems policy', *Foreign Policy*, 20 May 2010.

[8]   K. Kirişçi, 'Turkey's "demonstrative effect" and the transformation of the Middle East', *Insight Turkey*, 13(2), 2011, pp. 33–55.

[9]   See R. Menon and S. E. Wimbush, 'The US and Turkey: end of an alliance?', *Survival*, 49(2), 2007, pp. 129–144; M. Grufinkiel, 'Is Turkey lost?', *Commentary*, 123(3), March 2007, pp. 30–37; P. Zalewski, 'The self-appointed superpower: Turkey goes it alone', *World Policy Journal*, 27(4), Winter 2010–11, pp. 97–102.

[10] Yücel Bozdağlıoğlu, *Turkish Foreign Policy and Turkish Identity: A Constructivist Approach*, Routledge, London, 2003. See also P. Bilgin, 'Securing Turkey through Western-oriented foreign policy', *New Perspectives on Turkey*, 40(2009), 2009, pp. 105–125.

[11] Davutoğlu suggested that there was an unprecedented overlap in mutual interests. 'Obama Yönetimiyle Dış Politikamız Paralel', *Zaman*, 21 March 2009.

[12] Davutoğlu described the Arab Spring as the 'normalization' of history, which would enable the region to overcome the Cold War heritage of political autocracies and a psychology of enmity and distrust.

[13] O. Schlumberger, 'The ties that do not bind: the Union for the Mediterranean and the future of Euro-Arab relations', *Mediterranean Politics*, 16(1), 2011, pp. 135–153.

[14] Richard Gillespie, 'Adapting to French "leadership"? Spain's role in the Union for the Mediterranean', in F. Bicchi and R. Gillespie (eds), *The Union for the Mediterranean*, Routledge, London, 2012, pp. 57–76.

[15] 'EU response to the Arab Spring: new package of support for North Africa and Middle East', *European Commission*, Brussels, 27 September 2011, < http://europa.eu/rapid/press-release_ IP-11-1083_en.htm?locale=en > (accessed 5 March 2015); 'A new response to a changing neighbourhood', *European Commission*, COM (2011) 303, Brussels, 25 May 2011, < http:// eeas.europa.eu/enp/pdf/pdf/com_11_303_en.pdf> (accessed 5 March 2015).

[16] 'So close yet so far from safety', *UNHCR*, December 2014, < http://www.unhcr.org/ 542c07e39.html> (accessed 12 March 2015).

[17] G. Noutcheva, 'Institutional governance of European Neighbourhood Policy in the wake of the Arab Spring', *Journal of European Integration*, 37(1), 2014, pp. 19–36.

[18] R. Balfour, 'EU conditionality after the Arab Spring', *IEMed Papers*, 16(June), 2012, p. 26.

[19] R. G. Whitman and A. E. Juncos, 'The Arab Spring, the Eurozone crisis and the neighbourhood: a region in flux', *Journal of Common Market Studies*, 50(Annual Review), 2012, pp. 147–161.

[20] B. Nicoletti, 'Crisis upon decline. Foreign policy perspectives on the EU beyond the eurozone crisis', *ISPI Analysis*, 156(February), 2013, p. 2.

[21] N. Tocci, 'The European Union and the Arab Spring: a (missed?) opportunity to revamp the European Neighbourhood Policy', *IEMed Brief*, 2(June), 2011, p. 4.

[22] 'Turkey 2007 Progress Report', *European Commission*, SEC (207) 1436, Brussels, 6 November 2007, < http://ec.europa.eu/enlargement/pdf/key_documents/2007/nov/turkey_progress_ reports_en.pdf> (accessed 7 February 2015); 'Turkey 2014 Progress Report', *European Commission*, SWD (2014) 307, Brussels, 8 October 2014, < http://ec.europa.eu/enlargement/

pdf/key_documents/2014/20141008-turkey-progress-report_en.pdf> (accessed 7 February 2015).

[23] A. Frykholm, 'Obama and the Arab Spring', *Christian Century*, 128(12), 2011, p. 10.

[24] N. Hashemi, 'The Arab Spring, US foreign policy, and the question of democracy in the Middle East', *Denver Journal of International Law and Policy*, 41(1), 2012, p. 35.

[25] See on this, 'Remarks by the President on the Middle East and North Africa', *The White House*, 19 May 2011, <https://www.whitehouse.gov/the-press-office/2011/05/19/remarks-president-middle-east-and-north-africa%20 > (accessed 10 March 2015).

[26] D. Huber, 'A pragmatic actor—the US response to the Arab uprisings', *Journal of European Integration*, 37(1), 2015, pp. 57–75.

[27] Peter Jones, 'Hope and disappointment: Iran and the Arab Spring', *Survival: Global Politics and Strategy*, 55(4), 2013, pp. 73–84.

[28] H. Fürtig, 'Iran and the Arab Spring: between expectations and disillusion', *GIGA Working Papers*, 241(November), 2013.

[29] B. Aras and R. Falk, 'Authoritarian "geopolitics" of survival in the Arab Spring', *Third World Quarterly*, 36(2), 2015, pp. 322–336.

[30] B. Aras and E. Turhan, 'The "new Iran" must still grapple with old enmities', *Europe's World*, 28(Autumn), 2014, pp. 110–114.

[31] R. Dannreuther, 'Russia and the Arab Spring: supporting the counter-revolution', *Journal of European Integration*, 37(1), 2015, pp. 77–94.

[32] T. Schumacher and C. Nitoiu, 'Russia's foreign policy towards North Africa in the wake of the Arab Spring', *Mediterranean Politics*, 20(1), 2015, pp. 97–104.

[33] Aras and Falk, op. cit., p. 327.

[34] N. Redman, 'Russia's breaking point', *Survival: Global Politics and Strategy*, 56(2), 2014, p. 235.

[35] Shlomo Brom, 'Israel and the Arab World: the power of the people', in A. Kurz and S. Brom (eds), *Strategic Survey for Israel 2011*, Institute for National Security Studies, Tel Aviv, 2011, pp. 43–55.

[36] B. Berti, 'Seeking stability: Israel's approach to the Middle East and North Africa', *FRIDE Policy Brief*, 198, 2015.

[37] According to estimates, 15–25 per cent of foreign fighters involved in ISIS come from Western Europe and North America. See for details, D. Byman and J. Shapiro, 'Be afraid. Be a little afraid: the threat of terrorism from Western foreign fighters in Syria and Iraq', *Brookings Policy Paper*, 34, November 2014.

[38] Alastair Crooke, 'America immobilized as Iran–Saudi Arabia proxy war turns bloody', *Huffington Post*, 6 April 2015, <http://www.huffingtonpost.com/alastair-crooke/america-iran-saudi-war_b_7001776.html> (accessed 18 April 2015).

[39] Opposition parties criticized the JDP government's regional policy as dragging Turkey into the 'Middle Eastern swamp', a view shared by certain circles in the foreign policy establishment who advocate Turkish detachment. For a recent foreign policy debate along these lines, see 'Ortadoğu'ya bataklık demek ırkçılıktır', *Vatan*, 18 June 2014.

[40] For a bilateral arrangement along these lines, see B. Aras and E. Yorulmazlar, 'Turkey and Iran after the Arab Spring: finding a middle ground', *Middle East Policy*, 21(4), 2014, pp. 112–120.

[41] T. L. Friedman, 'Iran and the Obama doctrine—interview with President Obama', *New York Times*, 5 April 2015.

[42] For an argument on the irreversibility of the Arab transformation, see Paul Danahar, *The New Middle East: The World after the Arab Spring*, Bloomsbury Press, London, 2013.

[43] H. Mylonas and E. Yorulmazlar, 'Regional multilateralism: the next paradigm in global affairs', *CNN*, 14 January 2012.

[44] Kirişci, op. cit., p. 35.

[45] 'Erdoğan welcomes Iraqi president, calls ISIS a virus in Muslim world', *Daily Sabah*, 22 April 2015.

Emirhan Yorulmazlar is a Foreign Policy Institute (FPI) Fellow at SAIS, Johns Hopkins University. He was a former Harvard University WCFIA Fellow during 2011–12. He obtained his PhD from Bogazici University and MSc from London School of Economics (LSE). His research interests include Turkish foreign policy, Iran, the Middle East, US foreign policy and shifting balances in international relations.

Ebru Turhan is a Postdoctoral Research Fellow at Sabanci University's Istanbul Policy Center (IPC). During 2013–14, Turhan served as a Mercator-IPC Fellow in the thematic area of EU/German–Turkish relations. Her current research interests include EU–Turkish relations, Turkish and European responses to the Arab Spring, Germany in Europe and German–Turkish bilateral relations. Turhan obtained her doctorate degree in Political Science from the University of Cologne. Prior to joining IPC, she worked as a Senior Expert and Project Manager at the Berlin Representation of Turkish Industry and Business Association (TÜSIAD).

Index

Abdelmoula, E. 66–7
Abdulahad, Ghait 6
Abdullah, King (Jordan) 39
Abdullah, King (Saudi Arabia) 48, 62
advocacy 12
Afghanistan 76
Africa 24, 25, 27, 29, 30, 32, 33, 75, 76; North *see individual countries*
African Union (AU) 29
Agnew, J. 41
Ahmadinejad, Mahmoud 79, 82
al-Ahmar, Ali Mohsen 10
AKP Party 8
Al Jazeera 11, 49, 50, 64, 65, 66–7, 69, 70
Algeria 13, 93
Altunışık, M. 8, 9
ambassadors *see* diplomats/diplomacy
Anderson, B. 59, 60
Annan, Kofi 45
Apakan, Ertuğrul 33
Arab League (AL) 12, 29, 45
Aras, B. 9, 40, 78–80
arms control 30
ASEAN (Association of Southeast Asia Nations) 29
Asia 24, 30, 32, 33
Al-Assad, Bashar 7, 9, 14, 44, 45, 46, 47, 82–3, 84, 95, 99–100
asset recovery 67, 69
Association of Caribbean States (ACS-AEC) 29
asylum seekers 93
Atatürk, Mustafa Kemal 74, 81
Al-Attiyah, Khalid 11–12, 45
authoritarianism 1, 58, 91, 94, 95, 96, 99; Assad 47; Iran 74, 79, 81, 85, 95; military 77; orientalism 63–4; Qatar's geopolitical reasoning 41; resistance to 55, 56; status quo dynamics 38, 78; US foreign policy 94
autonomy 91
Ayubi, N. 57
Azerbaijan 101

Badawi, Raif 63
Bahrain 49, 55, 56, 64, 65; Al Jazeera 11; Iran 13, 14, 79, 96; mediation 6, 8, 13, 15; Saudi Arabia 63, 65, 96, 99; status quo dynamics 38; UAE 63
banking sector 44
Barakat, S. 12
Ben Ali, Zine El Abidine 57
bloggers 63
Bosnia 8, 41
Bouazizi, Mohammed 57
Bourguiba, Habib 59
Brazil 82, 84

capacity building and reform in Turkish Foreign Ministry 21–34; ideas and institutions 25–6; new geopolitics 22–5
capitalism, rent-seeking 78
Cem, İsmail 75
central country 23–4, 25, 26, 41–2
change, contextualizing dynamic of 57–63
chemical weapons 12, 45, 46, 94
China 73, 82, 83
Cole, J. 94
Comesa (East and South Africa Common Market) 29
computers and software 27
conflict resolution 41; mediation *see separate entry*
contextualizing dynamic of change 57–63
Council of Europe 30
Croatia 8
Crooke, A. 97
Çuhadar, E. 8
customs union agreement 94

Darfur 10
Davutoğlu, Ahmet 7, 8, 22–3, 24, 25, 26, 31, 32, 42, 45, 46, 48, 50, 75
de-securitization 22, 99
democracy 41, 55–6, 58, 74, 75, 76, 81, 84, 85, 98; Atatürk 74; definition 58–9; economic

and democratic reform 89; Egypt 12, 47, 48, 49–50; EU conditionality strategy 93; European Endowment for Democracy (EED) 93, 94; Gaza 42–4; Libya 6; military 77; Qatar 67, 69; Qatar's foreign policy 41, 42–4, 47, 48–9, 50–1; Saudi Arabia 62, 84; status quo monarchies 49; Turkey and EU 76, 77–8; Turkey's foreign policy 42–4, 47, 48, 49–51, 77–8, 92; Union for the Mediterranean (UfM) 92; United States 94; West as agent promoting 48, 50, 95
Derviş, Kemal 78
development assistance 7, 22, 49, 64, 66, 70, 85
dignity (*karamah*) 56
diplomats/diplomacy 29–31, 66, 75; ambassadors 27, 29, 31–2, 33; chequebook 41; diplomatic missions 24, 27, 30–4; humanitarian 74, 77, 85; international organizations 29, 33; multi-track style 31; number of 26; recruitment, education and working conditions 26–7
discourse analysis 40

e-consulate system 27
e-visa system 27
East Africa Community (EAC) 29
East and South Africa Common Market (COMESA) 29
economic cooperation 101
Economic Cooperation Organization (ECO) 29
economic development 77–8, 98, 100
ECOWAS (West African States Economic Community) 29
education 78
Egypt 9, 55, 56, 91, 92, 95, 99, 100; asset recovery 67; decline 8; foreign policymaking 66; geopolitical reasoning in Turkish and Qatari foreign policy 38, 39, 47–50; Israel 97; media 67; mediation 10; Nasser 59; Qatar 11–12, 39, 47–50, 64, 65, 67, 68, 69; Saudi Arabia 48, 63; status quo dynamics 38; Turkish model 77; UAE 63
embassies *see* diplomats/diplomacy
energy hub 101
energy security 93
Ennis, C.A. 11
Erdoğan, Recep Tayyip 6–7, 8, 42–3, 45–6, 48, 49, 50, 82, 84, 85, 100
Eurasia Economic Community 29
European Union 75, 90, 91, 92, 98, 100; budget for external action 93; customs union agreement 94; democracy: Turkey and 76, 77–8; migration 93; multicultural characteristic 24; Russia 96; Union for the Mediterranean (UfM) 92; US, EU and lost opportunity of Arab Spring 92–5
Eurozone crisis 93

Faisal, King 59
Falk, R. 40
Fatah 43
Fiji 9, 12
Foreign Ministry, reform and capacity building in Turkish 21–34; geographic reorientation 30–2; human resources 26–7, 28, 33; ideas and institutions: bridging the gap through capacity building 25–6; information systems 27; institutional reform 28–30
France 26, 73, 91, 92
Free Syrian Army (FSA) 45
freedom 56, 75
Freire, Paulo 56
Friends of Mediation 25, 29
Frontex 93

G-20 30, 76
Gaddafi, Mu'ammar 57, 59, 67, 69, 96
Gause III, F.G. 64
Gaza 10, 69, 70, 76; geopolitical reasoning in Turkish and Qatari foreign policy 39, 42–4
geopolitical panorama post-Arab Spring 95–7
geopolitical reasoning in Turkish and Qatari foreign policy 38–51; definition 40; discourse analysis 40; Egypt: political alignment and its limits 47–50; Gaza: similar foreign policy approaches 42–4; Syria: converging goals 44–7; threat–enemy chains 41, 51
geopolitics, Turkey's new 21–3, 32–4, 97–101; central country 23–4, 25, 26, 41–2; geographic reorientation 30–2; geographical replacement 24–5; human resources 26–7, 28; ideas and institutions: bridging the gap through capacity building 25–6; institutional reform 28–30
Georgia 8
Germany 26, 73, 84, 91
globalization 76–7
Gül, Abdullah 82
Gulf Cooperation Council (GCC) 13, 29, 48, 55–70, 93–4, 95, 96, 101
Gulf War (1991) 61

Hadi, Abdrabbuh Mansour 13
Hamad bin Jassim bin Jaber Al Thani, Sheikh 67
Hamad bin Khalifa Al-Thani, Emir Sheikh 10, 42, 43, 46–7, 48–9, 67
Hamas 10, 11, 15, 39, 42–4, 70
Hashemi, N. 94
al-Hashimi, Tariq 13
health care 78
Herb, M. 58
Hezbollah 13, 80, 81–2, 84, 97
Hobsbawm, E. 60
hostage cases and mediation 6, 8, 9, 10, 15
human resources 26–7, 28, 33

human rights 12, 30, 49, 82, 94
humanitarian assistance 7, 68, 69, 74, 76–7, 82, 85
Al-Humayd, Shaykh Salih Bin Abdullah 61
Huntington, S.P. 58–9

Ibn Saud 59
imagined communities 59–61
information systems 27
institutions and ideas: reform and capacity building in Turkish Foreign Ministry 21–34
international organizations 29–30, 33, 34; see also individual organizations
Iran 8, 40, 51, 57, 91, 95–6, 98, 99, 100; economic cooperation 101; Egypt 95; Hamas 42; hegemonic ambitions: Syria and Yemen 83–4; Israel 79, 80, 81, 82, 85, 97; mediation as foreign policy tool 4–5, 6, 8, 13–16; Middle East policy and divergences with Turkey in regional perspectives 78–80; nuclear programme 44, 73–4, 81, 82, 84–5, 91, 96, 98; Saudi Arabia 83, 84, 86, 96, 97, 98, 99; Syria 13, 14, 45–6, 47, 74, 79, 82–3, 95, 100; Turkey and Iran: two modes of engagement in Middle East 73–86; Turkish–Iranian relations 80–3, 85–6, 91, 96; United States 11, 73, 84–5, 96
Iraq 12, 39, 41, 44, 57, 66, 91, 99, 100; economic cooperation 101; federal system 99; Iran 14, 46, 80, 81; Kurdish people 81, 84, 91–2; mediation 6, 7, 8, 13, 14, 15
Iraq War (2003) 8, 61, 80, 91
Islamic Movement of Iraqi Kurdistan 80
Islamic State (IS) 9, 13, 39, 46, 51, 97, 100
Israel 8, 10, 15, 43, 44, 46, 57, 70, 91, 95; Iran 79, 80, 81, 82, 85, 97; wait-and-see approach 96–7
Italy 93

al-Jabouri, Salim 7
Jaish al-Fatah 83
Japan 66
Al Jazeera 11, 49, 50, 64, 65, 66–7, 69, 70
Jones, P. 14
Jordan 68, 97
Justice and Development Party (AKP/JDP) 22, 23, 43, 47, 48, 75, 81–2, 90, 91

Kamrava, M. 6, 65–6
Kerry, John 10, 44, 45
al-Khalifa, Shaikh Khalid Bin Ahmad 13
Khamenei, Ayatollah Ali 45–6
Khatami, Mohammad 81, 83
Koru, Naci 26, 27, 31
Kurdish people 81, 83–4, 85, 100; Kurdistan Regional Government (KRG) in Iraq 91–2, 97
Kuwait 55–6, 64

labour, foreign 12
language-learning opportunities 27

Lasswell, H.D. 58
Latin America 24, 30, 33, 76
least developed countries (LDCs) 25, 29, 30
Lebanon 9, 10, 41, 44, 47, 79, 80, 84
Libya 38, 39, 55, 77, 92, 100; asset recovery 67; European Union 93; media 67; Qatar 11, 12, 64, 65, 67, 69; Russia 96; Saudi Arabia 96; Turkey as mediator 6–7, 8–9, 15; United States 67, 94

Al-Maliki, Nouri 13, 84
Al-Marri, Ali bin Fetayis 67
mediation 4–16; Friends of 25; Iran 4–5, 8, 13–16; Iran: from expansionism to survival of the regime 14; Qatar 4–5, 9–13, 14–16, 41, 44, 66; Qatar: from ensuring stability to fostering change 10–13; Turkey 4–9, 13, 14–16, 25, 91; Turkey: from instituting order to preserving areas of influence 8–9
MERCOSUR (Southern Common Market) 29
Meshaal, Khaled 43
Michels, R. 58
migration 93
Moe, T.M. 26
Momani, B. 11
monarchical exceptionalism 63–9, 70
Morocco 56
Morsi, Mohammed 12, 48, 49–50
Moza bint Nasser, Shaykha 67, 69
Mubarak, Hosni 47, 56, 57, 66, 95
Mufti, M. 41
Muslim Brotherhood (MB) 10, 11, 14, 39, 42, 47–8, 49, 50, 51, 84
Al-Muslimi, F. 10

Nasser, Gamal Abdel 59
nationalism 59–61, 65, 81, 97; post- 76
NATO (North Atlantic Treaty Organization) 6–7, 30, 82, 96, 98
non-governmental organizations (NGOs) 23
non-interference principle 96
nuclear programme, Iranian 44, 81, 82, 84–5, 91; agreement 73–4, 85, 96, 98
nuclear security and Turkey 83, 85
nuclear terrorism 29
al-Nujayfi, Usama 7
al-Nusra Front 9, 83

Obama, Barack 94–5, 97, 98–9
OECD 30
oil and gas 65, 67, 69, 84, 93
Oman 13, 64
Öniş, Z. 9
Organization of Islamic Cooperation (OIC) 29, 30
Organization of South Asia Regional Cooperation (SARC) 29

orientalism 63–4
OSCE (Organization for Security and Co-operation in Europe) 30
Özal, Turgut 75

Palestine 8, 15, 48, 59, 66, 97; Gaza 10, 39, 42–4, 69, 70, 76
pan-Arabism 59, 66
Parsi, T. 14
PKK (Kurdistan Workers' Party) 91
poets 63
post-nationalism 76
private sector 78

al-Qaida 12, 61, 62
Qaradawi, Sheikh 50
Qatar 56–7, 59, 63, 69–70, 83, 100; dissidence 69; elections 67; explanatory dimension 65–6; geopolitical reasoning in Turkish and Qatari foreign policy 38–51; mediation as foreign policy tool 4–5, 6, 9–13, 14–16; monarchical exceptionalism 63–9, 70; orientative/normative map 68–9; programmatic angle 66–8; *Qatar National Vision 2030* 67–9

Ramsbotham, O. 5
real estate development 44
reform and capacity building in Turkish Foreign Ministry 21–34
refugees 68, 70, 82, 93, 98
regime change 44–5, 51, 96
regional integration 29
religion 60, 61, 62, 77, 78, 79, 80, 89
rent-seeking capitalism 78
al-Rishq, Ezzat 10
Robins, P. 90
Rouhani, Hassan 73, 83, 85, 86
rule of law 42, 58, 84, 94
ruling houses 58, 61, 64, 96; *see also individual countries*
Russia 8, 73, 82, 83, 93, 96, 99, 101

Şahin, M. 79
Saleh, Ali Abdullah 9–10, 13, 59
Salman, King 12, 65
al-Samarrai, Ayad 7
sanctions 85, 86
Saud bin Faisal 66
Saudi Arabia 39, 40, 47, 51, 57, 91, 99; counter-revolutionary 64–5; Egypt 48, 63; elections 62; foreign policy 66; Iran 11, 83, 84, 86, 96, 97, 98, 99; Libya 96; mediation 6; National Dialogue Forum 62; 'opposition'/'challenge' 61–3; al-Qaida 61, 62; Qatar 11, 12, 39, 41, 49, 50; religion and politics 61; Syria 47, 96, 98, 100; *takfeer* (relegation of fellow Muslim to the realm of unbelief) 62; traditional

charisma 59; US 11, 70; US airbase in Qatar 70; Yemen 46, 96
secularism 77, 81
Shanghai Cooperation Organization (SCO) 29
Shia Crescent 39
Singapore 66
Al-Sisi, Abdel Fattah 48–9
soft power: Qatar 11, 44, 66, 68, 69, 70; Turkey 8, 9, 24, 41, 44, 76, 77, 85, 90, 92
Somalia 76; -Somaliland 8
South Africa Development Community (SADC) 29
Soviet Union 75
special representatives 29
sports 70
subsidies 63
Sudan 10, 76
Syria 55, 81, 82, 86, 91, 94, 96, 98, 99–100; geopolitical reasoning in Turkish and Qatari foreign policy 38, 39, 44–7; Iran 45–6, 47, 74, 79, 82–3, 95, 100; Iran as mediator 13, 14; Qatar as mediator 9, 10, 11; Qatari funding of opposition in 11, 12; Qatari hosting of opposition 66; Qatar's foreign policy 68, 69–70; Turkey as mediator 6, 7, 8, 9, 15
Syrian National Coalition 45
Syrian National Council 45, 68

takfeer (relegation of fellow Muslim to the realm of unbelief) 62
Taliban 11
Tamim bin Hamad Al-Thani, Sheikh 48–9, 67
terrorism 29, 46, 49, 62, 84, 91, 93, 97, 98
TİKA (Turkish Cooperation and Coordination Agency) 22, 94
Tocci, N. 8, 94
Touval, S. 5
Tuathail, G. 41
Tunisia 39, 55, 56, 57, 65, 69, 77, 92; asset recovery 67; media 67
Turkey 68; autonomy 91; economic growth 76, 77; foreign policy: between Western orientation and regional disorder 89–101; foreign policy alignment with EU 94; foreign policy, major tenets of 75; geopolitics, Turkey's new *see separate entry*; Iran and Turkey: two modes of engagement in Middle East 73–86; Iranian–Turkish relations 80–3, 85–6, 91, 96; mediation as foreign policy tool 4–9, 13, 14–16; military 77; pre-Arab Spring foreign policy 90–2; reform and capacity building in Foreign Ministry 21–34; US, EU and lost opportunity of Arab Spring 92–5; zero problems approach 75–8, 90
Turks Abroad and Related Communities 22

Ukraine 96
Ulrichsen, K.C. 10–11
Union for the Mediterranean (UfM) 92
United Arab Emirates (UAE) 6, 11, 39, 49, 50, 63, 64
United Kingdom 6, 26, 73
United Nations 29, 30, 33, 66; asset recovery 67, 69; General Assembly 82; High Commissioner for Refugees (UNHCR) 7; Humanitarian Summit 29, 30; peacekeepers 9, 12; Security Council 25, 29, 33, 67, 73, 82, 84–5, 96, 98
United States 84, 90–1, 92, 96, 100; Bosnian War 41; diplomats 26; EU, US and lost opportunity of Arab Spring 92–5; Gaza 10, 44; Iran 11, 14, 73, 79, 84–5, 96; Israel 97; Libya 6, 67, 94; Obama doctrine 98–9; Qatar 10, 64, 67, 70; Syria 45

visas 27, 76

Wahabism 14
Wall, J.A. 5–6
welfare payments/welfarism 63, 64, 69
West African States Economic Community (ECOWAS) 29
women 63, 67
World Oil Congress 30

Yassin, Riad 13
Yemen 38, 39, 51, 55, 56, 96, 99; Iran 46, 74, 79, 83, 96, 98; Iran as mediator 13, 14; media 67; Qatar as mediator 9–10, 11, 12; Turkey 74, 83, 98; Turkey as mediator 6, 7–8, 9, 15
Yom, S. 64
Younesi, Ali 83
Yugoslavia 8
Yunus Emre Foundation 22

zero problems approach 75–8, 90

www.ingramcontent.com/pod-product-compliance
Ingram Content Group UK Ltd.
Pitfield, Milton Keynes, MK11 3LW, UK
UKHW010021280225
455677UK00023B/732